REV. E.L. BERTHON

Vicar of Romsey, 1860-1892

BUILDER
OF
COLLAPSIBLE BOATS

An Anthology

The Rev. E.L. Berthon

A portrait commissioned by his workforce, late 19th century

Photograph by English Heritage, by permission of Romsey Town Council

CONTENTS

Editor: Barbara Burbridge

3

Preface

The Reverend E.L. Berthon (1813-99) was one of Romsey's more flamboyant characters. As vicar for 32 years, he clearly took his calling seriously; parish records show him undertaking many pastoral duties. Hence, we are glad to include in this anthology a contribution about the parish from his successor, the present vicar of Romsey, Canon Neil Crawford-Jones.

Berthon oversaw much renovation of the Abbey church, and Frank Green, Heritage Officer of Test Valley Borough Council, has made a detailed study of this. Berthon harnessed his interest in scientific and engineering pursuits to the upkeep of his parish church, and his wider activities included the establishment of a boatworks in Romsey. When he retired in 1892, his workforce numbered more than a hundred men.

Romsey's local historians have long depended on Berthon's autobiography for details of his life and work. Then, on 21st August 2000, *The Guardian* reported that English Heritage had discovered a folding boat in an outhouse at Brodsworth Hall, Yorkshire. Our boat expert, Dr Jeff Hawksley, contacted the curator, Virginia Arrowsmith, and, hearing that a plaque on the boat read 'Berthon Romsey', went to visit Brodsworth.

Their subsequent collaboration led to much research on Berthon and his boats. Dr Hawksley's detailed model was included in the exhibition that English Heritage mounted, 2002-3, at Brodsworth Hall. In 2004, the exhibition was made available in Romsey for the summer. As a result of the publicity achieved by English Heritage, several people wrote in with stories about Berthon boats, and we are pleased to include some of their anecdotes, as well as some major studies of Berthon and his activities in Romsey in this volume.

Those who have contributed to finding out about Berthon and tracking down Berthon boats have had a lot of fun doing so. We hope that this book will enable you to learn about the man and that you will enjoy stories of his activities as much as we have done. We are grateful to Barbara Burbridge, the editor, for all the work she has undertaken in its writing and preparation.

Phoebe Merrick, LTVAS Chairman

INTRODUCTION

MR BERTHON'S TITLE TO FAME
Although a well-known clergyman, and one who was devoted to geographical, astronomical, and antiquarian study - he had a great affection for the famous Abbey Church, which he was never tired of describing - the deceased will be more widely known as the inventor of the collapsible boats, which are carried by many ships, and the making of which gives employment to so many persons in Romsey. The rev. gentleman also invented collapsible pontoons, largely adopted by the British and other Governments for military purposes, collapsible tents, which have been used in Polar exploration, and other things. As interested in the study of astronomy, he constructed more than one powerful telescope for the purpose of studying the Heavenly bodies.

Hampshire Independent, November 1899
(Report of the Rev. Berthon's Death)

The Reverend Edward Lyon Berthon, 1813-1899, was vicar of Romsey from 1860 until 1892, and then lived out his retirement years in the town. The story of his life – and the development of his collapsible boats – thus belongs essentially to the Victorian age. However, his son, who had long acted as manager of the Berthon Boat Company, continued to run the boatyard throughout the Edwardian period and on until his own death in 1917. After that the company was sold and moved away from Romsey.

Publicity about the 'rediscovery' of a 1909 Berthon boat at Brodsworth Hall attracted the attention of many people with a 'Berthon story' to tell. Much of the information gleaned from these sources has been included in this book.

This anthology is, however, mainly based on a series of talks prepared for a conference about him, planned for 24th April 2004. It enables the contributors to enlarge on their themes, and offers their work to a wider audience.

Editor

5

THE VICARAGE, ROMSEY.   Sillence. Photo.

Romsey Vicarage c1916
built in the 1850s
It was the Rev. Berthon's home for 32 years.
[now Folly House, a private residence]

THE LIFE OF BERTHON

Barbara Burbridge

'My family is descended from the *haute noblesse* of France.' So wrote the Rev. Edward Lyon Berthon on the opening page of his autobiography. This was published in 1899 by George Bell and Sons, London, under the rather Victorian title of *A Retrospect of Eight Decades*.

Berthon's proud assertion about his ancestry was justified but a trifle remote. Back in the 17th century, his great-great-great-grandfather had been the Marquis of Chatelléraut. The Marquis was a Huguenot, one of the fortunate members of that faith who managed to escape from France after the revocation of the Edict of Nantes in 1685. Seeking security, he fled to Portugal and settled in Lisbon. There the Marquis turned to trade, seemingly in the import-export business, and in this new context he decided to drop his titles, so that his son was simply St Pol le Berthon, businessman. The trade prospered and the family lived happily in Portugal for about seventy years, but then saw their home destroyed in the Lisbon earthquake of 1755. This disaster resulted in another change of country for at least one member of the Berthon family. This time the move was to England.

It was the Rev. Berthon's grandfather who settled in England, where he married into the higher echelons of the business community. His bride was the daughter of John Harrison, a director of both the East India Company and the Bank of England.

The area of the Berthon business interests expanded. There was now an excellent *entrée* by marriage into the English world of trade, and at the same time the links with Lisbon were maintained. During the Napoleonic Wars there was a particularly lucrative return for this dual aspect of the family concern. The Rev. Berthon's father, Peter, had contracts for supplying provisions to the British army in the Peninsula.

When Edward Lyon Berthon was born – the 10th child - on 20th February 1813, his parents were able to live in fashionable Finsbury Square, with a second home at Walthamstow (then a country locality). But this comfortable existence was disrupted a couple of years later when the business suffered a disastrous loss. A convoy of ships was wrecked off Portugal, and the family was reduced to comparative poverty.

This did not stop some of the Rev. Berthon's brothers and sisters from doing well in life. His eldest brother became secretary of the Trinity House, eventually drawing a pension of £1200 a year. Another brother became a captain in the Indian navy, while one of his sisters married Baron Alderson. So Berthon had good family connections among both ancestors and contemporaries.

He did not, however, enjoy a pampered childhood. Presumably for economic reasons after the business collapse, the young Berthon was cared for by his grandmother, who still had five unmarried daughters living with her. He described them as 'good relations, to whom I owe so much' but who sent him off to boarding school just before he was six – seemingly not knowing how to deal with a small lively boy in an all-female household.

He went to two schools that sound as if they could have been models for Dickens' *Dotheboys Hall*, his memories being centred around the poor food supplied and the extreme cold that he and his fellow pupils suffered. Even the learning that took place was endured rather than appreciated, for the emphasis was all on Latin, Greek and the arts. Mathematics and science, for which the young Edward Berthon had a natural talent and a keen sense of curiosity, did not feature.

He was rather better fed at his third school, but still did not excel at learning. Apart from drawing, his true talents lay outside the classroom. In his own time, particularly during the holidays, he records that he was making both an electrifying machine and a camera obscura; building model carts and carriages; and generally finding out about all sorts of scientific innovations. By this time his parents lived in Bangor, North Wales, and there, during holiday visits, he was able to watch and enjoy the construction of the elegant Menai Bridge.

Fortunately for Berthon, his headmaster was eventually persuaded by an influential parent to introduce mathematics and science into the school's curriculum, and at last Berthon began to earn academic respect. It was, however, only when he left school that he felt the need to redress eight lost years; he determined to learn Latin and Greek to a reasonable standard. This was because, within six months, he planned to follow his maternal grandfather into the medical profession, and realised that he would require a better understanding of Latin and Greek than he had so far achieved. Motivation saved the day: during the next six months he applied himself, and at last developed a life-long appreciation of the classics.

In the year 1828, at the age of fifteen, Berthon went to Liverpool, and there spent five years under the chief surgeon in the surgical wards of the medical institution. Those were the days before the introduction of anaesthetics, and Berthon records having assisted at gruesome amputations.

Because of the date and location of Berthon's medical training, he was in Liverpool at the time of the great railway competition at Rainhill, when three design engineers tried to sway developers to adopt their particular type of engine. Amongst them, of course, was George Stephenson, the eventual winner.

The event must have been irresistible for one of Berthon's insatiable curiosity about engineering and the sciences. He wrote, 'I consider it the greatest of the few honours I ever had, to be able to say that I stood by George Stephenson when he started the Rocket on the first mile of railway at Rainhill.'

He also felt privileged to have heard the great violinist, Paganini, when the latter was on a month's engagement in Liverpool. 'Like Orpheus, he so bewitched me, that I never missed hearing him one night during the entire month.'

After his five years in Liverpool, Berthon spent a year in Dublin to complete his studies at the College of Surgeons and to gain experience on the surgical ward of Meath Hospital. Before he left Ireland, however, he became a patient himself when he succumbed to acute pneumonia. He records being copiously bled according to the medical practice still prevailing in the 1830s. The whole experience left him very weakened, and unable to do more than undertake a prolonged convalescence. At the same time, his personal life changed radically.

At the age of nineteen, and while still in Liverpool, Berthon had met and fallen in love with Miss Margaret Preston, a connection by marriage. Following his illness, they married on 4th June 1834; he was just 21 years old. The pair then set off for a combined honeymoon and recuperation in Italy. They travelled in their own private coach, which some three years and several journeys later they sold to a cardinal in Rome.

Berthon never forgot those early journeys in Europe. 'How the railways have destroyed the charms of travelling', he wrote in the 1890s, though even then he still retained an unfaltering love of visiting other countries and immersing himself in their culture.

It was on his honeymoon journey that Berthon first thought in terms of navigational aids, but that story belongs to another chapter. He seems never to have practised as a doctor, except in emergencies.

He emerges from his recollections as a man of humour, who in his eighties was still remembering with amusement some of the pranks perpetrated by fellow students and himself. He was very much a European, and his enthusiasm continued lifelong. He was very keen on participating in the local culture and language of each country. In the early years of his marriage, he was able to afford the luxury of almost continuous junketing around the British Isles and the Continent, employing local people to smooth the path and wait upon his wife. He became perhaps a trifle snobbish about the increasing popularity of organised travel. His own independent and adventurous spirit and his energy are shown in his account of three hazardous ascents of Mount Vesuvius, once at night when the volcano was showing signs of activity. Only a day or so later, there was a full eruption, viewed by the Berthons from Sorrento.

Mrs Berthon, too, was made of sterner stuff than many. She journeyed to Ireland when six months pregnant, got thrown over a horse's head in a carriage accident and, proceeding from there to the Isle of Wight, gave birth to their first child in a draughty house at Ryde. It was now her turn to be the focus of a journey of recuperation. This time the Berthons went to Geneva, where they stayed long enough for a second child to be born – during a siege by French soldiers sent to recapture the escaped Louis Napoleon. Berthon seems to have stayed cool under fire, and even took time out for one of his rare medical forays, when he delivered a baby to a fellow countrywoman similarly stranded by events.

The Rev. Berthon sometimes used other people's diaries to help him remember crucial moments but was generally blessed with a good memory for his recollections, if not always for precise dates. He seems not to have kept a diary himself but his artistic talent led to a sketch-book record of his travels. Paintings by him of favourite views decorated his home in later years. Unfortunately, none is known to have survived.

Although the Rev. Berthon kept up his love of travel until only a short time before his death, the extensive and intensive travelling came to an end in 1841. By that time, at the age of 28, Berthon had determined to take Holy Orders. He duly went to Cambridge, and after obtaining his degree was appointed to the curacy of Lymington. Within two years he was presented to the living of Holy Trinity, Fareham, where he stayed some eight years.

Whenever health problems struck him or his wife, Berthon was allowed leave of absence to visit better climes – Bournemouth for three months and Jersey for six, for example. He also went on several pleasure excursions on the Continent, while at home he busied himself with his nautical devices, including his first attempts at promoting the idea of folding boats.

Berthon left Fareham in 1858 and, after a short temporary appointment, he accepted the living of Romsey, arriving in the town in 1860. For five years his life overlapped with that of Lord Palmerston, the Victorian prime minister who was also lord of the manor of Romsey. Berthon became a regular visitor at Broadlands, his lordship's country home on the southern edge of town.

Mrs Berthon's ill-health took them to the Mediterranean in November 1864, travelling with letters of introduction and advice from Lord Palmerston. Weeks on Gibraltar were followed by a spell on Malta, but sadly Mrs Berthon's health did not improve. At her request, they returned to Romsey in March 1865 and just one week later she died. Her death was followed in the autumn by another death – that of Lord Palmerston. This left the Rev. Berthon without his beloved wife and the supportive friendship of his chief parishioner. His undertaking of the renovation of Romsey Abbey provided an interest that must have been a great solace to him.

Astronomy provided an alternative interest, Berthon's absorption being sufficient to inspire his invention of a portable telescope. His love of travelling also continued, and later included a trip across the Atlantic. This journey had the added satisfaction of being in a White Star liner that carried six of his folding boats on board. He had developed the design of these boats over many years.

In the 1870s, with the encouragement of Samuel Plimsoll, Berthon began to make his folding boats commercially. He started with just 12 men working in a 100-foot long shed in the vicarage grounds, but soon moved onto a dedicated site to the east of the Abbey. The business was then put on a formal footing as the Berthon Boat Company, and grew so that eventually there were approaching 100 people on the payroll.

The principle of collapsible construction was extended to include marquees, bandstands and portable field hospitals, though these were produced in much smaller numbers.

Berthon Collapsible Bandstand c1880

A very disturbing element entered the Berthon family's life in the late 1870s, coming to a climax just as the vicar was establishing his boatworks on a formal basis. A well-kept secret has been linked to a newly arrived partner for a long-established legal practice.

Henry Cipriani Potter was an ambitious young solicitor, who, towards the end of the 1860s, bought a partnership with the existing firm of Stead & Tylee of Church Street. He quickly re-organised the offices, relocating them from the partners' private houses to separate property in Portersbridge Street. His efficiency is reflected in the well-kept records of the 1870s.

Amongst other clients, Potter advised the unmarried daughters of the Rev. Berthon, and strongly suggested that they should not allow their father to use their money for underwriting his new enterprise. This in itself must have been at least an irritation for Berthon as he attempted to raise funds for his ambitious business undertaking. But that would have appeared trivial compared with later developments. One of his daughters, Rosalie, ran away with Mr Potter, a disaster magnified by the fact that the flight left behind Mr Potter's wife and child. Thereafter, the census returns of 1881 and 1891 show only two unmarried daughters, Constance and Adela, living at home with the Rev. Berthon.

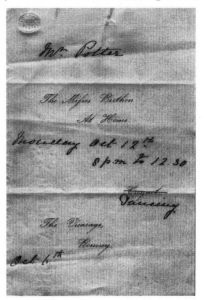

An Invitation to Mr Potter from the Misses Berthon before the elopement disrupted family life

With supreme tact the townspeople seem to have refrained from recording this shocking event in public, though there must surely have been considerable gossip in parishioners' parlours. The remaining legal partners severed all links with the disgraced Potter, and it is only in notes and documents about the dissolution of the partnership that any record of the whole sorry event is found.

Right at the end of his recollections, Berthon does imply a certain regret that he may have diversified too much. But he seems to have had a natural superabundance of curiosity, particularly about scientific matters, and a restlessness that found some satisfaction in constant travel.

The Rev. Berthon, 1889

His concern about diversification did not apparently cause him to worry about failing in his prime duty to the parish, and there was no obvious discontent amongst parishioners about his pastoral role as a vicar. There was, however, a challenge to his churchmanship during the 1880s, when considerable discord arose between the Vicar and the Abbey's Sunday School teachers about liturgical principles. Although his own memoirs suggest an animosity towards the Roman Catholic church as an organisation, Berthon adopted the ideas of the Oxford Movement, which supported the revival of Catholic doctrine within the Church of England as an antidote to perceived laxity. He gradually introduced new rituals that worried many of the congregation. Matters reached a climax in 1888 with the issuing of new regulations and obligations for the Abbey's Sunday School teachers.

One of these teachers was Mr Charles Moody of 13 Church Street (where the Moody Museum now forms part of Romsey Heritage Centre). He had taught in the Sunday School for over 23 years but, along with ten fellow teachers, was unable to accept the new rules, feeling that they were not compatible with the 39 Articles of the established church. It was a situation that distressed Mr Moody deeply. He kept various papers relating to this crisis, and they have survived.

Eventually the Sunday School teachers were dismissed for failing to comply with Berthon's changes – constructive dismissal in modern terms. Charles Moody changed his religious allegiance and joined the Nonconformists. In this he may have been encouraged by letters he received from outside Romsey after the dispute was given national coverage.

Responding, they declared, to one-sided accounts of the affair, Mr Moody and his fellow teachers issued the following press statement, which implies a determined inflexibility in the Rev. Berthon's attitude, unless it simply reflects exasperation at the ramification of diverging opinions.

THE FACTS RELATING TO THE DISMISSAL OF ELEVEN TEACHERS AND THE RESIGNATION OF THE SUPERINTENDENT OF THE BOYS' SUNDAY SCHOOL

A statement having been circulated that we were dismissed from the above school for teaching doctrines contrary to the teaching of the Church, we, the dismissed teachers, desire briefly to state the facts of the case, as enumerated below, and to deny absolutely the above untruthful and misguiding statement. We were called upon by the Vicar to sign a paper, containing three rules, by which we were to be bound:-

First:- To attend the Holy Communion the first Sunday in every month, either at 7 or 8 o'clock a.m.

Second:- To teach the children in our classes from a book which he had introduced into the school, or from books that may hereafter be introduced.

Third:- Compulsory attendance at an instruction class, to be held every Thursday evening, in the Abbey Church.

Having met together for the purpose of considering the foregoing rules, it was unanimously resolved that we could not subscribe our hands to them, and that a letter be written and sent to the Vicar, stating our reasons for non-compliance, which was accordingly done, and dated May 22nd, and signed by us, and to which we individually received the following reply:-

> Vicarage, May 23, 1888
>
> Dear Sir, - It is absolutely necessary that all the teachers in my Sunday Schools should conform to rules laid down by me, and I am sorry to say unless you subscribe to them, you will not retain your classes, which will be given to others next Sunday.
>
> Yours, faithfully,
> E.L. BERTHON

Now, with reference to the rules, our objections were as follows:-

First:- That we could not submit to compulsory attendance at a celebration of the Communion, administered with the following ritual: - Altar lights, mixed chalice, coloured stoles, &c., and the omission of half the sentences by the minister

15

when delivering the bread and wine to the laity, as by this act the sacrament is administered in the faith of transubstantiation, and, therefore, in direct opposition to the 28th Article of the Established Church of England.

Secondly:- The book put into our hands to teach contained the following Romish doctrines, viz., Invocation to the Virgin Mary, "bowing to the altar", making the sign of the cross; the bread and wine at the prayer of consecration, is changed into the body and blood of Christ; sacraments of marriage, confirmation, and penance; confession to the priests; "prayers for the souls of the departed", "purgatory" &c.

Third:- We felt, even if we had the time at our disposal, we could not attend the meetings (termed instruction meetings) to be taught such things as the foregoing, knowing them to be miserable delusions, and doctrines of the Church of Rome, and, therefore, contrary to the word of God, and the thirty-nine articles of the Church of England.

During the time it has been our pleasing duty to teach the children in our classes, we can conscientiously and fearlessly say we have taught nothing contrary to the inspired word of God and the doctrines as set forth in the Articles of the Church.

The move towards High Anglicanism may have alienated other parishioners, but there is no discernible indication of any objections to Berthon's absorption in nautical matters. People may just have been grateful for the employment that his boatworks brought to the town. In any case, once the business was established, the Reverend's son was responsible on a day-to-day basis, and Berthon himself was less directly involved.

If few examples of parishioners' expressed views of Edward Berthon as a vicar can be found, there are certainly several instances of the esteem in which he was held within a wider context. He was incorporated at all levels of society; on one hand he had the friendship of Lord Palmerston, while on the other he was president of the Romsey branch of the Hampshire Friendly Society throughout the whole of his time in the town.

Just two years after the Rev. Berthon's appointment to Romsey, there was a high-profile exhibition in the town. Reports about this event show how quickly the new vicar became a well-known local figure. The 1862 Romsey Exhibition was the town's attempt to emulate the Great Exhibition of 1851. It was a very high status event. Lord Palmerston opened the exhibition on St George's Day. Exhibits were loaned by the local gentry, by Winchester Cathedral, Winchester College and Winchester City Museum, as well as by the great and the good of Romsey and the surrounding district.

Model boats were part of a display, and may reflect the Rev. Berthon's nautical interests. The exhibition was supplemented by a series of talks and concerts, and Berthon featured strongly as a speaker. He was already a widely recognised figure in navigational matters.

Photograph of Model Boats at the Romsey Exhibition
taken by Cllr Slater, chemist, and his assistant, Mr Frost, 1862

Later, in the final decades of the 19th century, the Berthon boatworks also brought admiration at all levels. His own workforce subscribed to the expense of a splendid portrait of their employer in later years. This was renovated in the 1980s with the support of the Berthon Boat Company of Lymington. It now hangs in the Council Chamber of Romsey Town Hall and is flanked by the related illuminated address, on long-term loan from Romsonian Mr Terry Viney.

Even more impressively, the boatworks received a special visit from the much admired Victorian explorer, Henry Stanley, the man who uttered the immortal words, 'Dr Livingstone, I presume' on discovering the missing missionary doctor in the depths of the African jungle. Mr Stanley, marrying at a mature age, interrupted his honeymoon in the Test Valley to come to Romsey, folding boats being popular for river navigation in difficult terrain. Special demonstrations were laid on for him.

Rather amusingly, many of the townsfolk turned out to see the illustrious visitor. Expecting that the Rev. Berthon would bring him to visit his church, quite a number forked out the requisite 6d to enter the Abbey, only to be disappointed by Mr Stanley's non-appearance there.

After being vicar for 32 years, the Rev. Berthon retired in 1892. He had to vacate the vicarage but continued to live in Romsey, where he enjoyed seven years of retirement before his sudden death in late October 1899; he was 86 years old.

The coffin of the Rev. E.L. Berthon lying in Romsey Abbey framed by the screen that he created from original medieval fragments

The lengthy eulogy in *The Hampshire Independent* was most appreciative. It noted that 'Romsey people, to whom he was so familiar, can hardly realise that he is gone, for only 13 days before he died he was in his loved Abbey Church, and read the Lessons in his well-known sonorous voice.'

About his sudden final illness – due to a chill – it continued 'He only kept to his bed entirely for a day or so, and as late as Wednesday last week he was sitting up and chatting brightly and interestedly about current events, and especially about the [Boer] war, the stirring episodes of which he followed on a map before him. His intellect, which had always been so marvellously astute, was clear to the very last ...'

The younger people in the town could not remember any other incumbent in their parish church. A great many valued the improvements he had made to their parish church and even more appreciated the way in which he had brought new hope and pride to the town itself through his engineering talents.

The many floral tributes at the funeral of Edward Lyon Berthon on 2nd November 1899 included one with the following message from his workforce, 60 of whom followed the cortege:

> *From Employees of the Berthon Boat Co., who have lost a kind master and a true friend, but he will always live in our memories. With sincere sympathies*

Lower Section of Berthon Memorial Window, Romsey Abbey
Photograph courtesy of English Heritage
by permission of the Vicar of Romsey
~~~~~~~~~~~~~~~

Sources
Berthon, Rev. E.L., *A Retrospect of Eight Decades*, George Bell & Son, London, 1899
Hampshire Record Office: *Tylee, Mortimer & Attlee Collection*
LTVAS Records
Members of the Berthon Family, including:
        Mrs Louise Stewart Cox
        Vice Admiral Sir Louis Le Bailly
The Moody Papers in the care of King John's House & Tudor Cottage Trust (Romsey Heritage Centre) & LTVAS
The Hampshire Independent of 9th August 1890
The Hampshire Independent of November 1899

Cover of Illustrated Berthon Catalogue c1902
Courtesy of King John's House & Tudor Cottage Trust
(Romsey Heritage Centre)

20

BERTHON REDISCOVERED: The Unique Story of an Edwardian Berthon Boat

Virginia Arrowsmith, English Heritage

Historic View of Brodsworth Hall, Yorkshire
Photograph courtesy of English Heritage

An Unexpected Find

An old generator house in the grounds of a Victorian country house in South Yorkshire was, in August 2000, the unlikely location of a unique discovery. Amongst what one might expect to find in a disused outhouse was a folded Berthon boat of characteristic wood and canvas construction, identified by the brass plaque on the gunwale.

Berthon Boat Company
The plaque on the
gunwale of the boat
Photograph courtesy of
English Heritage

Bugs and Beginnings

Having languished in the damp for many years, the boat was – and is still - in a very fragile state. English Heritage treated the boat immediately in order to eradicate insect pests in the wooden components, pioneering a new technique of heating objects up to 52°C.[1]

21

Reference to the boat, in an article in *The Guardian* about this new treatment, caught the interest of Phoebe Merrick, chairwoman of the Lower Test Valley Archaeological Study Group from Romsey in Hampshire. Thus began an incredibly exciting journey of investigation, which inspired much new and important research.

Excitement at the English Heritage find was due in part to the fact that few of these boats were known to be still in existence, although several more in museums and private collections around the country have indeed come to light as a result of the 'rediscovery' of the Brodsworth Berthon boat.

In addition to the immediate conservation concerns, the question on everyone's mind was how such an unusual boat had come to end its days on a country estate in landlocked South Yorkshire. Visually unremarkable, with its perished canvas skin, faded wooden gunwales and struts, its appearance belied the intriguing story behind its invention, a story that will unfold in the following chapter by Jeff Hawksley.

The Berthon boat on display at Brodsworth Hall
Photograph courtesy of English Heritage

Historic context and intended use
Although Berthon's collapsible boat had initially been designed for use as a lifeboat, the 'collapsible' principle was soon modified and adapted for an extensive range of other equally successful uses.

Fishing in a Berthon boat
From the Berthon Illustrated Catalogue, courtesy of King John's House & Tudor Cottage Trust (Romsey Heritage Centre)

Of robust construction yet surprisingly lightweight, the laminated Canadian rock-elm structure and skins of waterproofed flax canvas rendered it ideal for a series of popular leisure uses. Its compact design and folding mechanism, governed by an elaborate series of hinges, enabled the ribs of the boat to fold up like the leaves of a book. The separate watertight compartments created by a double-skinned construction gave the boat remarkable buoyancy even when damaged, for if one compartment was punctured the others still remained buoyant, a useful feature in any nautical scenario, where damage to a single-skinned boat could prove disastrous.

Part of a Berthon 'Duplex' boat loaded on horseback
from the Berthon Illustrated Catalogue, courtesy of King John's House & Tudor Cottage Trust (Romsey Heritage Centre)

The floor, mast, rudder and rowlocks were all detachable, enabling the boat to be stowed in confined contexts and ensuring remarkable ease of carriage. Some boats could in fact be packed up so small that they could be carried on a man's shoulders or on horseback.[2]

This combination of minimum weight, portability and strength made Berthon's boats eminently suitable as tenders on pleasure craft, and undoubtedly accounts for their popularity with the yachting fraternity at the turn of the last century. Among these yachtsmen could be counted Charles Thellusson of Brodsworth Hall.

23

The Brodsworth 'Berthon'

Charles Thellusson (1860-1919) was the third son of Charles Sabine Augustus Thellusson, who built the new Brodsworth Hall in the early 1860s. Charles inherited the family estate in 1903, both of his elder brothers having died without issue. Like his father and brothers before him, he was a keen yachtsman.

Charles and his wife, Constance, owned property in Torquay (Devon) and a steam yacht, the *Carmela*, which had been purchased at some considerable expense by Charles' brother, Herbert, shortly before his death in 1903.

Charles and Constance Thellusson who bought the Berthon boat in 1903
Photograph courtesy of English Heritage

Charles and Constance spent many months yachting on the south coast, during which time they may well have learnt of the existence of Berthon's invaluable little boats. They also explored the coastlines of Northern and Western Europe in the early years of the twentieth century.

The invoice for the Brodsworth boat, dated 17th April 1909, was identified, shortly after the 'rediscovery' of the boat, among receipted bills and estate papers in the Brodsworth archives.[3] The invoice was presented on elaborately headed paper identifying the Berthon Boat Company as: *Sole Manufacturers of the Berthon Boats, Canoes and Tents. Contractors to the Home and Foreign Governments. Also to all the leading Shipping Companies.* It records the purchase of a '12ft Berthon dinghy complete. £18.18.0'. The boat was sold with a mast and sail costing an additional £1.15s., an extra half gallon of paint, a

24

repair bag and slings, with sling hooks, the total costing £21 14s.3d.

Swimming around the Brodsworth 'Berthon'
Photograph courtesy of English Heritage

It seems probable that Charles and Constance only used the Brodsworth 'Berthon' for a short time before the way of life they enjoyed, so typical of their social class, was irredeemably shattered by the impact of the First World War. Oral accounts relate that, on hearing news of the outbreak of war in July 1914, the Thellussons instantly aborted their stay at a hunting lodge on the Isle of Harris, where their twin pleasures of yachting and shooting were amply indulged, and returned to Brodsworth without even collecting provisions for the journey home.[4]

Shortly after the end of the war, in 1919, Charles Thellusson died and the Berthon boat became redundant, since his younger brother, Augustus, who inherited the estate, preferred shooting to yachting as a leisure pursuit. On his death in 1931, the estate passed to his nephew, Charles Grant-Dalton.

The Generator House Brodsworth Hall
Photograph courtesy of English Heritage

In 1940, the boat was taken down to the generator house, which was no longer required after the installation of mains electricity in that year. Wilf Hindle, son of the last estate foreman, described how, as an eight year old, he had excitedly pretended to row across the Atlantic in the boat when Charles Grant-Dalton and his father had moved it – and its many component parts - to the brick outhouse.[5] This seems to have been the last time the boat was opened, and it is unlikely that it was used again.

The Brodsworth 'Berthon' was popular in its heyday
Photograph courtesy of English Heritage

Condition and Conservation

Having been stored for sixty years in a damp outhouse, there was concern about the structural condition of the boat. The fragility of the perished canvas, in its unconserved state, precluded the possibility of opening the boat, which had been stored in the closed or 'folded' position throughout that time.

Research in the Patent Drawings Section at the British Library, however, yielded new information on the composition of the flax canvas coating, which will serve as a starting point for future conservation work. Berthon's 1886 patent describes in detail the composition of the waterproofing substance, containing a mix of linseed oil, boiled soap, terebine (a turpentine solution from the terebinth tree), and 'spruce yellow ochre'.[6] This unique solution had to combine four essential components for it to successfully meet the requirements of the boat, namely water resistance, lightness of weight, flexibility and durability. The turpentine, as a hydrocarbon, will have acted as a solvent, solubilising the soap, and aided by the linseed oil, used to establish a water resistant base, made up a thick, 'soupy' solution that was easy to apply. The turpentine solution will additionally have hastened the drying out process of the oil.

The inclusion of soap in this intriguing solution puzzled the English Heritage historic paint specialists. The reaction of the sodium in soap (sodium stearate) with the turpentine and linseed oil may have worked together to act as a mordant, binding the solution to the flax canvas. In addition to its role chemically, soap may also have introduced flexibility into the composition, vital for maintaining the pliability of the canvas when folding. The spruce yellow ochre, ground in oil and mixed with the boiled linseed oil, seems most likely to have been added as a colorant. This solution would have given the canvas a much lighter brown appearance than the dull grey seen today.

The unique mixture was developed not only for waterproofing purposes but to make the canvas more durable in conditions across the British Empire, many parts of which were being explored in Berthon Boats by the 1890s. Berthon proudly boasted that this coating was both 'rat and termite proof' and was, as such, 'world-wide climate-proof'.[7] Conservators at the Textile Conservation Centre, based at the University of Southampton, have indeed recognised the potential for an innovative research project on historic waterproofing solutions, their compositions and deterioration processes.

Some of these deterioration processes are sadly, but not unexpectedly, already at work on the Brodsworth boat. Several of the components of the waterproofing solution may have begun reacting against each other, responding differently to temperature and humidity. The animal glue, used to join the laminates of the stem and sternpost, has long since begun to destabilise, causing the bond to weaken and the laminates to start opening up. In 2002, when the boat was brought into Brodsworth Hall for display, care had to be taken to ensure that these deterioration processes were not hastened by placing the boat in a drier environment. English Heritage conservators advised on acceptable temperature and humidity parameters, for an object of wood and canvas construction.[8] The room in which the boat was displayed was monitored regularly to ensure that no significant fluctuations in temperature or humidity were occurring, a matter of concern in a building which had been noticeably drying out in the previous 15 years.

Having been heat-treated for pest eradication when found, the boat was surface-cleaned, a process that also served to prevent further abrasion to the painted wooden structure or coated canvas. The galvanised steel components (rowlocks, pins, bolts and fixing holes) were brushed to break down the superficial corrosion caused when such a coating is damaged, the consequent exposure of the bare metal to humidity resulting in surface corrosion. The metal fixings were therefore waxed with a microcrystalline wax to form a protective barrier against moisture ingress.[9] In all, these basic measures of preventive conservation care served to ensure that the boat's condition did not deteriorate significantly following its removal from the generator house, ensuring a more secure future for one of the most unusual items in the English Heritage collections.

Survival and regeneration

The story of the Brodsworth boat is not only a testament to the design and construction of a unique and remarkable object but to the processes that affected its survival over almost a century. Brodsworth Hall was gifted to English Heritage in 1990 by Pamela Williams, one of the last surviving members of the Grant-Dalton family. The contents were purchased by the National Heritage Memorial Fund on behalf of English Heritage, and every object retained until its function, historic value and relevance could be reasonably established. The value of making a holistic and informed judgement on the collections as a whole, and as a collection of individual items, has been highlighted by stories such as this: new information has come to light and indeed new identifications have been made possible, sometimes many years later. An apparently humble object, like the Berthon boat, which initially presented itself as something of an anomaly, has, as this research project has revealed, left a significant legacy on present times, not just in terms of its contribution to improved safety at sea, but in the revolutionary design and construction that set a precedent for inflatable equipment and waterproofing materials prior to the widespread use of gum and rubber in the twentieth century.

Berthon as portrayed in memorial window
Photograph courtesy of English Heritage

Ultimately, the rediscovery of the Brodsworth boat has inspired a regeneration of interest in the life and work of the Rev. Berthon: it has not only brought an object back to life but has highlighted the foresight and practical genius of a man whose great contributions to society were not justly recognised or rewarded in his own lifetime. They are, it is hoped, celebrated here at last.

New Discoveries

A number of additional component part of the Brodsworth Berthon boat were identified subsequently. These included the folding floor and interlocking seats, features that had been anticipated for this model based on knowledge of similar sized boats, as depicted in Berthon's original drawings. Hinged along the centre line, the boards could be attached to fixings on the lower two ribs of the boat. The floor also provided the anchor points for a pair of additional struts, which gave added rigidity to the structure in open position. When the boat was closed or 'folded' for stowage, the hinged floor and seats would fold along the centre line or could be removed.

Constance & Charles in their other collapsible boat
Photograph courtesy of English Heritage

A large expanse of structured canvas, waterproofed with a similar solution, was also found in the same location as the boat. Initially assumed to be a cover for the 12-foot boat, assessment of its physical structure and analysis of photographic evidence has, remarkably, confirmed it to be another collapsible boat, although it is as yet unclear as to whether or not it is of Berthon construction. It was found complete with detachable hinged gunwales and rowlocks, which, through a series of locking steel brackets, would have given rigidity to the whole. Although its condition again precludes the possibility of opening the structure out, it is hoped that future research will positively identify the boat and its original design and function

NOTES:
1. A. Xavier-Rowe, D. Imison, B. Knight and D. Pinniger, 'Using Heat to Kill Insect Pests – Is it Practical and Safe?', *Tradition and Innovation: Advances in Conservation, IIC 18th International Congress, 2000*, London, pp206-11.
2. Berthon Boat Company, *Illustrated Catalogue and Price List*, 1902, pp.20, 22, 26 (King John's House & Tudor Cottage Trust: Romsey Heritage Centre)
3. Brodsworth Estate Accounts, (uncatalogued) Doncaster Metropolitan Borough Council Archives
4. Oral History Interviews with Mrs Christina Edwards, 1993 and 2003.
5. Oral History Interview with Wilf Hindle, 2002
6. Patent no. 5936, 1886, British Library Patent Drawings Section.
7. Bournemouth Graphic, 15th March 1906, p172, Portsmouth RO; *Illustrated Catalogue and Price List*, p23
8. The advised range of relative humidity for a composite object of wood, metal and textile construction is 45-65%.
9. (various) Report on the Brodsworth Hall Berthon Boat, (unpublished), De Montfort University, 2001, pp1-4

Special Note: The issues presented by the discovery of the Berthon boat are further discussed in the Collections Review (Vol. Four, English Heritage, 2003)

Berthon Boats came in a variety of sizes generally ranging from 7ft to 28ft
*from the Berthon Illustrated Catalogue
courtesy of
King John's House & Tudor Cottage Trust (Romsey Heritage Centre)*

LETTER TO THE TIMES, 28th April 2002

following publicity about the Brodsworth Berthon boat, and indicating that Berthon was not alone in thinking of ways to ensure passengers' safety at sea

From Miss Kay Bowen

Sir, The Berthon collapsible boat (report, April 13; letters, April 20), made in response to an 1849 shipping disaster, was of elm. An inflatable rubber boat, invented by Lieutenant Peter Halkett in 1843, could double as a cloak when not inflated.

P.A.L. Vine relates in *Pleasure Boating in the Victorian Era* (Phillimore, 1983) that it was tested on the Thames in 1844 and thought by the Admiralty to be useful for explorers and surveyors but not for the Navy. It was used by the Arctic Land Expedition in 1846 and later manufactured under Halkett's direction by Samuel Matthews, of Charing Cross.

Courtesy of Miss Kay Bowen and Mr P.A.L. Vine, author of Pleasure Boating in the Victorian Era

Picture 1
Hussars packing up Berthon Boats for Transport
from the Berthon Illustrated Catalogue c1902
courtesy of
King John's House & Tudor Cottage Trust (Romsey Heritage Centre)

32

Berthon's Collapsible Boats

Jeff Hawksley

The Rev. Berthon was a remarkable man; churchman, inventor, engineer and astronomer. But probably his most important achievement, and the one for which he is best remembered, was his invention of the Berthon Collapsible Boat.

Although his boats were widely acclaimed in his later years, his initial attempts to popularise his invention were less successful. In his autobiography *A Retrospect of Eight Decades*[1] he separated the two periods devoted to the Collapsible Boat into his First and Second Innings. His first, from about 1850 to 1856, was played in Fareham, where he was the vicar at Holy Trinity Church. It was marked by disappointment and he set his ideas aside until 1873 when he came in to bat once again. This time he succeeded, and the boat-building company he founded continued for some time after his death until his son also died in 1917, after which the boat-yard in Romsey finally closed.

Berthon's objective was to produce a lifeboat to be carried aboard ships and it may be useful, here at the outset, to look back and see how ships, and shipping, changed and developed during the first half of the 19th century.

When Berthon was born in 1813, all ships were built of wood. Very few were larger than 1000 tons and sails were the only means of propulsion, although several important experiments with steam engines had been undertaken by this time. Already there was an awareness of the need to make better arrangements to help save the lives of passengers and seamen when ships foundered by storm or stranding. Many ships had run onto rocks close inshore, often within view of local people, who were condemned to watching the sufferings at sea while being unable to offer any assistance. It was after one such distressing incident in 1789[2], when the ship *Adventure* went aground near the River Tyne, that a group in South Shields formed a committee to address this question: they raised a subscription to offer a prize for a design of a suitable inshore lifeboat. The committee formed the nucleus of what would later become the Royal National Lifeboat Institution, and the prize was won by Henry Greathead. Within four years 23 of his boats were distributed around the coast plus another eight abroad.

Ships had, of course, long carried small boats on board but the purpose of these was not primarily to save lives in the event of shipwreck. They were provided to carry passengers and crews, water and stores, between the ship and the shore. They were usually stowed on the deck near the centreline where they had some protection from breaking seas, but they were in no way handy for launching in an emergency.

The First Innings.
By 1850, when Berthon embarked on his campaign, ships were being constructed in larger sizes. Wooden ships were still being built but iron ships were becoming more common. Many were fitted with steam engines but they still retained a full sailing rig of masts, spars and sails to conserve coal when the wind was favourable and to provide driving power when the engines broke down. These newer ships were no longer so dependent on the vagaries of weather and they were able to offer reliable liner services, especially between Britain and the United States. It was a time when huge numbers of people were moving around the world - emigrants to the U.S.A. and Australia, administrators, merchants, settlers to the Colonies and troops, especially to India. Many of the old wooden sailing ships were pressed into service. They carried cargo in the lower holds and emigrants in the tween-decks on the outward journey, returning with full cargoes of cotton, timber, wool and other commodities. Quite small ships could carry 200 emigrants or more. But as ships grew in size the numbers of passengers and crew carried on board similarly increased and the scale of disaster was magnified in proportion. Berthon recognised this.[3] He also recognised that most ships did not carry sufficient boats to accommodate all aboard should an emergency strike. Nor could they. Clear decks were essential on sailing ships for handling the sails and at this time all ships had sails.

Berthon was finally persuaded of the need for improved life-saving arrangements on board ship by the loss of the *SS Orion*[4] off the Scottish coast by Portpatrick on 18th June 1850. *Orion* was an iron paddle steamer of 510 tons built in 1846 or 1847. She ran a regular service between Liverpool and Glasgow, and on her fateful last voyage she was northbound out of Liverpool with about 200 people on board.

Picture 2: **Wreck of the *S.S. Orion*** from a drawing by the Rev. Berthon as published in his *Retrospect of Eight Decades*

Very early in the morning she ran onto rocks and sank in 15 minutes. She was close inshore but, even so, while some were saved by the ship's own boats and more were picked from the sea or from the rigging by local boats setting out from the shore, around 45 lives were lost. Saddened by this disaster, Berthon hit on the idea that if boats could be folded up so that they occupied less space then more boats could be carried; enough to accommodate all hands aboard. This is where the story begins. But the opportunity will be taken here to give a description of his invention, how the boats were built and how they folded up.

Berthon Collapsible Boat
Fig. 1

Drawn by G.J.Hawksley
Romsey, September 2003

Figure 1 is a sketch of a small Berthon Boat. The design of this example belongs to Berthon's Second Innings but, apart from the detail of the hinges, boats built in the early years were very similar. Of a total production of several thousand boats only a few were built during his Fareham years and it is probably more relevant to use the later design for this explanation. Looking at *Figure 1* there are three ribs (some of the larger boats had four) on either side of a central keel. They run from end to end and they are connected to the stem-post and the stern-post by a clever chain hinge, patented by Berthon in 1873[5].

The ribs are built up from laminations of thin strips of wood, bent to shape by steaming, and then fastened together with glue and bolts. Because the grain of the wood follows the curvature of the rib and runs along its full length a very strong assembly is formed. This construction was ideal for his boats and Berthon was clearly so experienced and confident with the technique that he used the same principle for the beams in the roof of the North Transept of Romsey Abbey. They are still there to be seen today.

In the assembled, or working position, the ribs stand apart in radial planes shown more clearly in *Figure 2*.

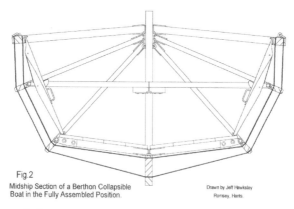

Fig.2
Midship Section of a Berthon Collapsible
Boat in the Fully Assembled Position.

Drawn by Jeff Hawksley
Romsey, Hants.

The floor and the seats are made in two halves hinged along the centre-line and to the ribs at either side. In this assembled position both the floor and the seats lie flat, pushing the ribs outward and giving the boat transverse rigidity. Struts support the gunwales and in this way a strong, rigid framework is formed which is covered with two layers of waterproof canvas spread over the ribs. Effectively this makes a boat within a boat. The double skin arrangement provides a second line of defence if the canvas is pierced, and air trapped in the compartments formed between the ribs gives added buoyancy.

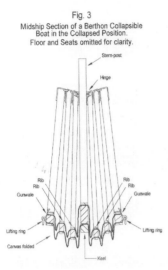

Fig. 3
Midship Section of a Berthon Collapsible Boat in the Collapsed Position.
Floor and Seats omitted for clarity.

To fold the boat the struts are released and the ribs fall down like the pages of a book as shown in *Figure 3*. At the same time the floor and the seats fold up as shown in *Figure 4* and this illustrates an important feature of these boats; there are no loose parts to be lost or misplaced as they are all connected together by hinges. *Figure 5* is provided to illustrate the action of the struts. These are very clever and they also form a part of the patent of

1873. In the process of assembling the boat the levers of the struts are located into the lugs on the gunwale and then levered downwards. This stretches the canvas tight and finally the levers snap into place to form rigid struts to support the structure as described earlier. These are the features that characterise all Berthon Boats.

One of the problems associated with Berthon's First Innings is to establish a time scale and the problems begin right at the outset with the sinking of the

Fig.4
Midship Section of a Berthon Collapsible Boat in the Collapsed Position.
Ribs omitted for clarity

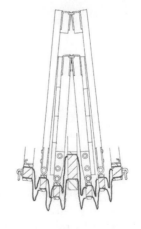

Orion. In his autobiography, *A Retrospect of Eight Decades*, written only shortly before his death in 1899, he acknowledged this sorrowful catastrophe as the inspiration for his idea and he

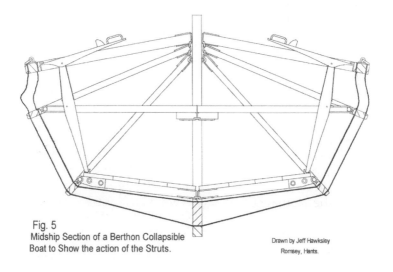

Fig. 5
Midship Section of a Berthon Collapsible
Boat to Show the action of the Struts.

Drawn by Jeff Hawksley
Romsey, Hants.

gave the date as 29th June 1849. By implication this marked the beginning of his endeavours. He also wrote 'The very next day I made my first collapsible boat and took it to Portsmouth Dockyard, when the admirals and officers, in a 'Return' to the House of Commons[6], reported on it in high terms'. In fact, the *Orion* sank on the 18th June 1850, so already the story is a year out of step. Further, the 'Return' to the House of Commons, which did indeed report in high terms, was dated 28th June 1854 and referred to a boat 'now in progress of construction by the Rev. E.L. Berthon of Fareham'. Recognising the frailty of memory, no criticism of the Rev. Berthon is implied. But untangling the story, and setting it to a believable timescale is an intriguing problem. Many difficulties have been encountered along the route and many uncertainties remain.

What is known of his First Innings? In July 1853, Berthon published *The Fareham Lifeboat*,[7] a nicely produced little book, setting out the advantages of his collapsible boat. In this book he referred to a boat 21 feet long and 7 feet wide, which he started building in 1850 and finished in the winter of that same year. This boat had been tried on H.M.S. *Sampson,* and over 40 years later Admiral Thomas Saumarez reported that he had

38

been First Lieutenant on the ship in 1852 and had been favourably impressed by Berthon's boat. Also in *The Fareham Lifeboat,* Berthon referred to a model he entered at the Great Exhibition of 1851, where it gained a prize. But 'being placed on a stand with no one to exhibit it, its peculiarities appear to have been seen only by the jurors'. There is also a mention in *The Fareham Lifeboat* of a small boat just 17 feet long. He called it a gig and recommended it for use as a tender for a yacht.

Other articles appeared in the *Nautical Journal* in 1852[8] and in *The Lifeboat* magazine in 1853.[9] In 1854 Berthon brought out a pamphlet, also published in Fareham, called *Berthon's Patent Collapsing Lifeboat.*[10] To a large extent they all covered the same ground. But the pamphlet included a reprint of the 'Return' to the House of Commons which, as mentioned earlier, was dated 28th June 1854. So the pamphlet must have appeared after this. Precise attention to dates becomes important now.

In his later writings Berthon was justifiably pleased by the intervention of Queen Victoria in promoting his ideas to the Admiralty. In his *Retrospect[1]* he gave the date of his audience as 1852 and in his lecture to the Royal United Services Institution in 1895[11] he said that the Queen and Prince Albert had viewed his boat '42 years ago'. Subtraction gives 1853. It is surprising that he did not mention this important event in his earlier publications.

On 1st September, Berthon wrote a letter to Captain James Anderson of Hallam Hill, Titchfield[12] saying, 'I have just received the intimation of the Prince's wish to inspect the boat <u>tomorrow</u> and I write in haste to beg your kind and valuable services on the occasion...'. Unfortunately, the year is missing from the dateline. From his *Retrospect* we learn that he received the Queen's command while sailing his boat on the Serpentine on a Friday. He was to present the boat at Osborne the next day, i.e. Saturday. Again no year is given. But on the 2nd September 1852 the Queen was in Scotland and in 1853 she was in Dublin. However she was at Osborne on 2nd Sept 1854 and in that year the second of September was a Saturday. There is no mention of the meeting in *The Times* nor has any record been found in the Royal Archive. Nevertheless, 1854 is plausible and the following sequence is offered.

On 10th July (again no year) Berthon wrote again to Capt. Anderson:[13] 'I am going to put the boat in the water on Thursday about 2 p.m. Will you come and take an early lunch here a little before one and if you will give me the benefit of your advice about sails etc. I will be very much obliged'. Berthon had also given Capt. Anderson a copy of *The Fareham Lifeboat*. This copy is now in Portsmouth Record Office and contains the inscription 'Captain Anderson R.N. with the author's kind regards, June 1854'. In the margins around one of the pages Capt. Anderson has written some notes regarding the choice of sails and refers to the launch of the boat on 13th July 1854. The entry was dated 18th July 1854. Capt. Anderson had also received a copy of the 'Return' to the House of Commons and had written notes on the back which include 'On the 22nd July, whilst sailing in her, I ran alongside the *Excellent*'.[14] At that time *H.M.S. Excellent* was a wooden warship moored in Portsmouth Harbour and used as a gunnery training school. 'Eighty hands from *Excellent* came into the boat which, with seven of our number was equal to 87. This trial of buoyancy was considered very satisfactory.' It is very likely that the boat Capt. Anderson was sailing was the 30-foot boat which was 'now in the progress of construction' on 19th May 1854 when the Master Shipwright at Portsmouth Dockyard prepared his report for the 'Return' to the House of Commons.

The boat being ready and in working order in July, there would have been ample time to transport it to London, and for it to be sailing on the Serpentine when Queen Victoria's command arrived in September. Following his audience with the Queen, Berthon recorded that Prince Albert wrote to the Admiralty suggesting that they buy a couple of boats for appraisal. No record of this letter, or the order placed by the Admiralty, has yet been found, but the next step appears in a letter from Berthon to Capt. Anderson[15] dated August 19th. As usual no year is given but the sequence of events suggests this must now be 1855. In this letter Berthon thanked Capt. Anderson for past favours received and reported that a boat-builder in Rotherhithe was building two 32-foot launches. Capt. Anderson wrote in the margin 'The boats to be built by B. for the Admiralty are to be

32 ft. by 9ft. 6ins. for which he is to have £150 each'. In the same letter Berthon added 'Thus far I have a good start and do not doubt the perfect success of the scheme'. But he also wrote that the India Rubber makers had raised the price to such an extent that there would be no profit left. It is clear that at that time he was using India rubber to waterproof the canvas. Ironically, as would become apparent much later, it was the use of rubber that led to much of the prejudice against his boats and one of the reasons why his hopes for 'the perfect success of the scheme' were not realised.

Among Captain Anderson's papers at Portsmouth Record Office[16] is a fine pencil sketch, drawn by him, of a Berthon boat, 30 feet long and illustrating his proposals for the sails. Handwritten notes on the back are dated March 1855. Presumably the drawing was made in response to Berthon's earlier request for advice. Capt. Anderson was obviously an authority on sailing rigs for small boats and there are many more of his sketches, equally beautiful, in the Record Office in Portsmouth. Berthon made special claims[7] for the sailing qualities of his boats. He explained that the pressure of water outside caused the canvas to bulge inwards to form longitudinal furrows. These, he claimed, increased the resistance to sideways motion without impeding headway and so improved performance when sailing to windward.

Of the two 32-foot boats delivered to the Admiralty in 1855[1] one was sent to a Guardship at Sheerness for evaluation. Unfortunately, the report was unfavourable despite the fact that, as Berthon recalled in his *Retrospect*, a Howitzer had been put aboard and many rounds had been fired successfully. The *Lifeboat* magazine of 1st July 1857[17] reported similar trials with artillery on a Berthon boat. These had taken place 'about two years ago', i.e. some time in 1855. The boat was described as an experimental mortar-boat and it is not clear whether this was one of the two 32-foot boats already mentioned or another constructed specially for trials with a mortar. The boat sank after firing several rounds but this was attributed to damage sustained when the mortar was being hoisted aboard. It may be wondered why a small boat should be expected to carry heavy guns. At that time ships' boats were regarded as an extension of a ship's operating reach in battle and they may also have needed defences when approaching hostile shores. At any event, it was a requirement that all Naval boats should carry guns and no exception appears to have been allowed for Berthon's. The same magazine article gave news of a Berthon boat carried aboard the Troopship *Perseverance*. On previous reasoning, it could well have been in use for two years. Despite everything, the final verdict on Berthon's boats was unfavourable and hopes of orders from the Admiralty were dashed. Attempts to interest Merchant shipowners were equally disappointing. [1] He did, however, receive an order for six huge boats, each 50 feet long, for the *Great Eastern*, a ship of enormous size, far larger than anything attempted before, or for many years to come. Her keel was laid down in May 1854 and she was launched in January 1858.[18] This must have been a most exciting order for Berthon. But, after completing only one, the order was cancelled. He received payment only for the work done and the one boat he built languished in Southampton for many years because there was no other ship big enough to use it. Discouraged, he gave up the struggle and his First Innings came to an end. He took a long lunch break and didn't come in to bat again until 1873. By this time he had moved to Romsey and this was where his Second Innings was played.

The Second Innings.
Berthon's second attempt to popularise his collapsible boats began in 1873, thirteen years after taking up a position as the vicar of Romsey Abbey, and he acknowledged the support of Samuel Plimsoll[1] who encouraged him to make this new start. Plimsoll had been elected to Parliament in 1868, and he was passionate in his campaign to improve ship safety. It was largely through his efforts that the Merchant Shipping Act of 1875 was passed with new regulations to limit the load a ship could carry. All ships had to be marked with a 'Load Line', indicating the maximum loaded draught, and this is still known affectionately as the 'Plimsoll Line'.

In the run-up to Plimsoll's bill there had been a number of dreadful disasters at sea; two were especially poignant. In 1873, the *Northfleet*[19], a fine sailing clipper, had sailed from London outward bound with emigrants for Tasmania. While lying at anchor off Dungeness, she was struck by a passing ship and sank in 30 minutes with the loss of 293 lives. The following year the *Cospatrick*[2], another sailing clipper, caught fire off the Cape of Good Hope and was lost. She, too, was carrying emigrants to Australia. Of a total of 473 passengers and crew, only 3 were saved. These tragedies came at the time that Plimsoll was raising public awareness, and in this climate Berthon received a better reception.

During the years that Berthon had allowed his interest in boats to rest, ships had increased in size yet again. In 1873 the *City of Richmond*[18], 4600 tons, entered service to carry about 1500 passengers between Liverpool and New York. The following year two important transatlantic liners were launched for the White Star Line, the *Britannic* and the *Germanic*.[18] Each could carry over 1200 passengers plus 130 crew. Such huge increases in size, and in passenger numbers, further increased the potential for catastrophic losses in the event of an accident, and there was still an urgent need for ships to be better equipped with lifeboats. Berthon set about filling this need and in 1873[1] he engaged six carpenters and six shoemakers (he believed boat-builders to be too restricted by the traditions of their craft). He then built a shed about 100 feet long in the vicarage garden and started work.

Having made a new start, he was quickly rewarded with a substantial order for boats for the Indian troopships. The order was placed by Admiral Sir William Mends,[11] the Director of Transports, and his support was important. In 1876, Berthon read a paper to the Royal United Services Institution [R.U.S.I.],[20] and Mends contributed to the discussion. He regretted the earlier rejection and '... I can assure you all, that I shall sleep more soundly in my bed when I feel that all troopships are carrying boats capable of accommodating the whole of the people they convey. These Indian Troopships carry 1650 to 1700 souls while their boats and rafts will only take 800 ... The Board of the Admiralty and the Secretary of State for India in Council viewed it, as their duty, and ordered these boats to be built and supplied to all troop ships'.

Lord Alfred Churchill, another contributor to the discussion following Berthon's paper to the Royal United Services Institution, had recently crossed to New York in a large passenger liner. It was 450 feet long and carried '10 boats of the ordinary construction. But these were either fitted on chocks or upon booms and were so fitted that in the event of a sudden emergency it would be 10 to 1 if they could be used at all. There were 1,350 on board, 1,000 emigrants plus 350 First Class passengers and crew'. Here was another example of the difficulty of stowing sufficient lifeboats without cluttering the decks and of the vulnerability of larger ships with greater passenger numbers.

In the same discussion, Churchill asked whether the canvas cracked when the boat was folded for a long period. Berthon assured him this did not happen due to the action of the soap '... surprisingly this does allow the paint to dry and it dries rapidly'. It is interesting to examine this question of waterproofing the canvas because it goes some way to explaining Berthon's lack of success in his first innings. In 1873, the year when the *Northfleet* was lost, an exhibition of marine safety equipment was staged and Berthon entered one of his collapsible boats. In the same discussion, the Chairman revealed that he had been one of the referees at the *Northfleet* exhibition and that they had rejected the boat because they considered that the skin, treated with india rubber, was unsuitable. He recognised that Berthon now used a different preparation, and this was clearly the case. In fact Berthon had said, early in his lecture, 'The first impression of a canvas boat is understandable prejudice against that treacherous gum called caochouc or india rubber and this has retarded the adoption of my invention by a quarter of a century. If the Royal Navy and the Merchant Navy had expressed any interest in the boats, an alternative would have been sought and found, as indeed it has been'. Could it be that all his earlier efforts had been rejected for such a simple reason?

Soap was mentioned in Berthon's reply to Lord Churchill above and this must have been an important ingredient. But it was not until 1886, as a part of Patent number 5934,[21] that the full specification for his waterproofing compound was published. In any event, he must have introduced the new treatment very soon after starting his Romsey enterprise as he had, after all, given the Admiralty the confidence they needed to place their order. It was this order that gave Berthon his start and he grasped the opportunity with such enthusiasm that, shortly after

44

his death in 1899, a correspondent to *The Times* could write[22] 'His reward came at last however and he lived to see the value of his noble endeavours fully recognised. The Berthon boat is now used by the Army, the Navy, the mercantile Marine, by Arctic explorers, by travellers all over the world and by owners of pleasure craft'. It only remains to add detail to this elegant summary.

Berthon's success in supplying boats for the Indian troopships has been mentioned, and in 1895[11] he could report 'I am now engaged in executing orders by which all her Majesty's Troopships will be abundantly supplied'. And, in his *Retrospect*, he could add that four to six of his boats 28 feet long had been on every ship that carried British soldiers ever since that first order. But he quickly realised that his boats could be supplied for other markets. Eight early 'Berthons' accompanied General Gordon who, between 1874 and 1876, was exploring the upper reaches of the Nile. In 1875, Admiral Sir George Nares took two small boats, seven feet long, on his expedition to the North Pole, and Frederick Selous used two for his voyages on the Zambezi. Berthon was now able to justify his claim that the canvas, and its waterproofing compound, could withstand extremes of temperature from the Tropics to the Arctic. An early example of a specialised application was the construction of a boat to carry the end of a transatlantic telegraph cable to a beach in America from the cableship *Faraday*[23]. This was in 1874 and must have been very soon after he had started up in Romsey. No doubt encouraged by these early successes, the Rev. Berthon[24] formed the business into a limited company, *The Berthon Boat Company Limited, in 1877;* his son, Edward Pearson Berthon, was Manager.[25]

When Berthon read his paper to the Royal United Services Institution in 1876,[20] he was still unhappy that the owners of emigrant ships were doing little beyond what the law required in providing lifeboats. However, a daring voyage was arranged. In 1882,[26] Captain Frederick Harvey and a crew of five, including William Turner, a boat builder employed at the Berthon Works in Romsey, launched a 28-foot boat from the liner *Essequibo* in mid-Atlantic some 400 miles west of the Lizard. From there they sailed back to Southampton, a distance of 700 miles, to demonstrate the seaworthiness of the boat. William Turner was, unfortunately, seasick for most of the time. A similar demonstration was undertaken in 1890,[27] when another 28-foot boat named *Berthon* was sailed from Southampton to Liverpool, a distance of 525 miles, in 71 hours (see Picture 3). Whether these demonstrations had any influence is not known, but the Company Catalogue, published around 1902,[27] had an impressive list of customers including most of the larger shipping companies.

Picture 3
25ft Berthon boat leaving Southampton for Liverpool
19th May 1890
from the Berthon Illustrated Catalogue, courtesy of King John's House & Tudor Cottage Trust (Romsey Heritage Centre)

Captain Harvey, of the Atlantic sailing adventure, had previously invented a type of torpedo. It never came into use, however, as an improved 'locomotive', or self-propelled, torpedo had been introduced by Robert Whitehead around 1865. Whitehead's torpedoes were gradually improved, and by 1877 the Admiralty had a new class of very small, and very fast, torpedo-boats under construction for launching them. These torpedo-boats were only 11 feet wide and Berthon was asked to produce boats that would fold up into a small enough parcel to allow them to be stowed inside.[11] The result was the 'Duplex' construction and

150 boats were built for the Admiralty and a further 650 for the French and other navies.

Picture 4:
9ft Duplex boat
showing the join midway under the rower's seat
from the Berthon Illustrated Catalogue, courtesy of King John's House & Tudor Cottage Trust (Romsey Heritage Centre)

The Duplex was clearly a successful variant of the Berthon folding boat. It was built in two halves, divided at the midship section, and each half was a self-contained boat. The arrangement became popular for military use, where the sections were small enough, and light enough, to be carried by a pony.

Similarly, they could be carried to remote lochs and rivers for fishing. J. Edwards-Moss in his book *A Season in Sutherland,*[28] published in 1899, sent to the Army and Navy Stores for a 9-foot Duplex collapsible boat and 'with immense labour he transported his purchase on a deer pony to the loch. He came miserably home at the end of a weary day with just three minnows'.

Picture 5: **7 ft Berthon Boat at Unst Boat Haven, Shetland**
Photograph by Jeff Hawksley

The Army and Navy Stores catalogue for 1907 had boats for loch and river fishing. A 9-foot boat cost £12 and a Duplex of the same size was £14. Although not a Duplex, the little 7-foot boat now in the Unst Boat Haven in Shetland and shown as *Picture 5*, is thought to have been bought for just this purpose around 1882.

47

Half a Duplex on end with other half folded in front beside a set of basic 'Berthons' in folded position

A 20-foot Quadripartite 'Exploration' Duplex ready to sail

Both above pictures from the Illustrated Berthon Catalogue, courtesy of King John's House & Tudor Cottage Trust (Romsey Heritage Centre)

48

Britain now had the torpedo and the torpedo-boat to launch it. And, judging by production figures, so too did France and other nations. Inevitably, the next step was the 'Torpedo-boat Destroyer'[29] to destroy the torpedo-boats. Introduced around 1892, these were larger, around 185 feet long, but still very narrow. Berthon boats were specified as standard equipment and 'hundreds' were supplied. As late as 1902, *The Romsey Advertiser*[30] could report that 30 boats, 20 feet long, had been ordered for Her Majesty's Torpedo catchers. Seven hundred Berthons had been supplied to the French Navy and it is possible that some of these were used to bring relief and supplies during the Paris floods of 1910.[31] A series of postcards showed sailors from Dieppe handling Berthon Duplex boats at that time. Another naval success was the provision of collapsible boats for Patrol-boats.[32] Sixty-four of these were built in the First World War and each carried four 20-foot Berthons.

Berthon was certainly successful in supplying boats for Naval use but he was also promoting his boats for military purposes. By 1876[20] two huge boats, 40 feet long, had been delivered to Portsmouth for evaluation. They were designed to carry a field gun, horses and 60-70 men in various combinations. He had also considered using his boats as pontoons and recommended 'Very excellent bridges of all sizes, and to carry all weights, from men in single file to the passage of the heaviest siege train or elephants can be made on this plan ...'.

To demonstrate his ideas he built a pontoon bridge over the River Test and 'our Volunteer Corps passed over'. A demonstration at Runnymede[1] for the Royal Engineers met with the same resistance he had previously experienced with his lifeboats. Once again, the canvas construction was the stumbling block, and Berthon's protestations that a footbridge made up of 14 small boats had been used in the Zulu War of 1879 failed to persuade them. The Prussians, however, ordered 230 pontoons, each 22 feet long, built in three sections on the 'Tri-partite' principle.[11] He did succeed in the end and, addressing the Royal United Services Institution in 1895, he reported that the British Army had bought his boats but they preferred his two-part 'Duplex' model. The idea of boats built in sections was extended even to a 'Quadripartite' boat in four sections,[27] two pointed ends and two rectangular mid-sections.

Bow and stern sections together made a boat 11 feet long, two ends and one middle made a boat 15ft 6ins long and all four made a boat 20 feet long. It was, apparently, popular with travellers and explorers and a 22-foot model was used by the Army as it could be carried on a light cart.

Picture 6: **A Quadripartite Duplex**
from the Illustrated Berthon Catalogue, courtesy of King John's House & Tudor Cottage Trust (Romsey Heritage Centre)

Another military application involved swimming horses across rivers. In his address to the R.U.S.I. in 1895,[11] Berthon described how 'Eight troopers, in two lines, rode into the river, four on each side of one of the boats. They dismounted on board with their saddles, arms etc. Two men at the stern then shoved the boat into the stream; the horses walked until they could no longer touch the bottom and then, by swimming, they crossed the river and the pontoon (now effectively an 8 horse-power boat) travelled, without rowing, at a good speed'. Captain Ferguson, in the discussion following the address, reported that, in one manoeuvre, a horse plunged around in the water and put a hoof through the outer skin and scratched the inner skin. A handkerchief over the hole allowed another 30 or 40 horses to cross. But the men's feet got wet. In this same address Berthon also described how small Duplex boats could be carried on pack horses or mules for building light bridges etc. About 90 small boats, nine feet long, had been supplied to the Royal Engineers,[27] of which 36 had been sent for use in the Zulu War of 1879. A bridge built up of 14 of these boats has already been mentioned.

Picture 7: **Cavalry Crossing the Thames**
from the Illustrated Berthon Catalogue, courtesy of King John's House & Tudor Cottage Trust (Romsey Heritage Centre)

Berthon's eventual success in persuading the naval and military authorities to accept his boats and pontoons was clearly the result of persistence. The resulting sales must also have been beneficial to his firm. Yet, during his address to the Royal United Services Institution in 1895,[11] and having offered to arrange a demonstration in 1895 to prove the superiority of his boats for use with heavy guns, he says 'I leave it to other heads and hands to make this warlike application. My province and aim is to produce a lifeboat and not a death boat'. This is a surprising remark to make to an audience of the highest ranking naval and military officers.

What of their peaceful uses? Their popularity with anglers and explorers has been mentioned but his catalogue[27] also recommends them for duck shooting in India as 'the sides can be lowered when approaching the ducks'. There is another story,[33] not typical but certainly unusual, about Samuel Cody. On 5th November 1903, Cody embarked on a novel adventure using a kite to tow a Berthon boat across the Channel. He had intended to make the crossing from England but, because of an unfavourable wind, he had to take the ferry to France and then sail the boat and the kite back from Calais overnight. He arrived safely at Dover at 8.30 the next morning.

Berthon boats were also promoted as tenders for yachts and steam launches. At this time wealthy Victorians were sailing some quite ostentatious yachts and the Thelluson family,[34] of Brodsworth Hall in Yorkshire, had some of the largest ever built. It is possible that the Berthon boat found at Brodsworth had been purchased in 1909 as a yacht tender.

And, continuing the theme of sporting applications, Berthon applied the folding principle to the production of a line of canoes.[35] A number of these survive and they are of a

particularly elegant design, as shown in Picture 8. Testimonials in the Berthon catalogue[27] suggest he had satisfied customers as far apart as Brazil and India. At home, a special advantage claimed for them was that they shut into a width of only four inches and so they could be carried in the luggage van of passenger trains for which, if a charge was made, it was only for excess baggage. Obviously this was an important consideration.

Picture 8
Replica 10ft Canoe
Photograph by Jeff Hawksley

Berthon's competitors should be mentioned. One such competitor was Cunnah Wright & Co., who built dinghies stuffed with reindeer hair.[29] Berthon received a setback in 1894, when the standard boats for H.M. Torpedo Destroyers were switched from Berthon's to Cunnah Wright's. But, after only one year, Berthon regained the contract and his boats continued to be specified for some years to come. For ship lifeboats, a design produced by Engelhardt,[36] a Danish company, offered strong competition. The Danes, indeed, produced collapsible lifeboats, and more will be said of them shortly. Another was the 'James' collapsible boat,[37] although there seems to have been a friendly rivalry between Capt. James and the Rev. Berthon, for, in 1894 the Berthon Boat Company challenged James to a race. The course was from Southampton, around the Bell Buoy off Cowes and back to Southampton and the stake was £100. It is sad to report that the Berthon boat lost by 18 minutes and 23 seconds. However, in the discussion following the R.U.S.I. paper of 1895,[11] Capt. James reported that he owned a Berthon boat and he spoke very highly of its strength and durability. James's boat had only one skin and, referring to another contribution at the same meeting, he suggested that if a rent could be stopped with a handkerchief why bother with a double skin?

Some measure of Berthon's success can be gained from the ships he supplied. The *Spartan*[1] of the Union Steamship Company had one 25-foot boat, one of 22 feet, one of 14 feet and one of 10 feet. Berthon took a trip to South Africa on this ship in 1881 when she was quite new. The s.s. *Teuton* of the same line had a Berthon while the *Teutonic* of the White Star Line had six Berthons, each 28 feet long. The *Empress of Ireland*[38] had four Berthons in addition to 16 regular lifeboats and 20 collapsible boats by Engelhardt. Closer to home, the *Stella*,[39] a ferry operating between Southampton and the Channel Islands, carried two cutters, two lifeboats, a dinghy and two Berthons. Unfortunately the *Teuton*, The *Empress of Ireland* and the *Stella* were all lost. They sank very quickly with serious loss of life and there is no record whether the Berthons were used effectively. In the case of the *Stella,* one Berthon boat was launched but it is uncertain whether it was incorrectly assembled or whether it was swamped.

A question sometimes asked is whether the *Titanic*[40] carried Berthon boats. The answer is no. But she did have four collapsible boats made by Engelhardt and they saved many lives. However an unusual story unfolded when the *Titanic's* sister ship, the *Olympic,* arrived back in Southampton the following week.[41,42] To reassure the passengers, the company put 24 Berthon boats on board so that these, plus the regular lifeboats already on board, would accommodate all hands. This, of course, had been Berthon's objective all along. But the firemen – the men who tended the fires in the boilers – found one of the boats was damaged and refused to sail. The ship, now short of firemen, had to delay her departure for New York and anchored in the Solent. Next day a demonstration was arranged for the firemen and they were satisfied, provided the faulty boat was replaced. In the meantime a number of inexperienced firemen had been recruited to replace the strikers and, as a result, some 50 sailors now refused to sail with them, claiming they would be unable to cope in an emergency. The upshot was that the sailors were tried for mutiny in Portsmouth, found guilty but released without punishment and the ship missed a voyage.

The *Titanic* disaster was something of a turning point for the Berthon Boat Company. It benefited in the short term as, in addition to the 24 boats supplied to the *Olympic,* further orders were received to bring the total up to 300.[24] But, quite soon afterward, the regulations governing ship's lifeboats were changed and Berthon boats no longer met the specification. After the death of Edward P. Berthon in 1917 the firm was sold to Henry May who had, at that time, just purchased a boatyard in Lymington. May closed the Romsey works shortly afterwards. This must have been a disappointment for the town; at its peak around 1899 the yard had provided employment for 100 men. It had a reputation as a good employer and had a profit sharing scheme[43] which must have been something rather special in those days. The closure of the works signalled the end of an important chapter in Romsey's history.

The preceding paragraphs make rather sad reading and it would be well to quote a few cases where Berthon boats have proved their worth. In 1885, when the Navy sent one of the 32-foot boats to the Guardship at Sheerness for evaluation towards the end of the First Innings, Berthon left his own 20-foot boat on loan with them. News reached the Guardship that a fishing smack had gone aground in a gale some three miles away and was sinking. Berthon's 20-foot boat was launched and rescued three men and a boy. This was probably Berthon's first success and he was very pleased to receive the news. In 1902,[44] a German torpedo boat was in collision with the steamer *Firsby* off

Cuxhaven. Sir Edward Birkbeck, then the chairman of the Royal National Lifeboat Institution, the Hon. Rupert Guinness, Somers Somerset and a servant were on board the torpedo boat. This had a Berthon boat on board, and it was used to carry the honourable gentlemen, together with five German sailors, to the safety of a lighter. Another, slightly earlier, torpedo boat story is quoted in the Berthon catalogue of 1902. 'The steersman and two engineers of the French torpedo boat No 21, which capsized in June 1895, were saved by the Berthon boat of French torpedo boat No 119.' Only these three cases have been found so far. There could well have been many more. In 1899 the correspondent to *The Times*[22] wrote of '... the Berthon Collapsible boat of the present day which is so universally used and has been the means of saving so many lives'. The Reverend Berthon could not wish for a better last line.

∿∿∿∿∿∿∿∿∿∿∿∿∿

References.
1. Berthon E.L., *A Retrospect of Eight Decades*, George Bell & Sons, London, 1899
2. Shaw Frank H., *Famous Shipwrecks*, Elkin Mathews & Marrott Ltd., London, 1930
3. Berthon E.L., *Five Boats in Place of One* in *The Nautical Magazine and Naval Chronicle*, 1852, page 118
4. *The Times*, Thurs. 20th, Fri. 21st June, Sat. 22nd and Mon. 25th June 1850
5. British Patent No. 1384, 1873
6. *Berthon's Collapsing Lifeboat; Return to an Order of the Honourable House of Commons*, dated 19th June 1854 with handwritten annotations by Captain James Anderson. Portsmouth Record Office, Hewitt Collection, Reference 16A
7. Berthon E.L., *The Fareham Lifeboat*, George Sutton, Fareham, 1853
8. Berthon E.L., *The Fareham Lifeboat*, The Nautical Magazine and Naval Chronicle, 1852, page 156
9. *New Inventions – The Fareham Lifeboat*; The Life-Boat, Journal of the National Life-Boat Institution, October 1853, page 70
10. Berthon E.L., *Berthon's Patent Collapsing Lifeboat*, George Sutton, Fareham, 1854

11. Berthon E.L., *Collapsible Lifeboats and Pontoons for Military Purposes,* Journal of the Royal United Services Institution, 1895, pages 359-381

12. Letter written by E.L. Berthon to Capt. James Anderson dated 1st September, Portsmouth Record Office, Hewitt Collection reference 16A

13. Letter written by E.L. Berthon to Capt. James Anderson dated 10th July, Portsmouth Record Office, Hewitt Collection reference 16A

14. Padfield P., *Rule Britannia*, Pimlico, London, 2003

15. Letter written by E.L. Berthon to Capt. James Anderson dated 19th August, Portsmouth Record Office, Hewitt Collection, reference 16A

16. Portsmouth Record Office, Hewitt Collection, reference 16A

17. *The Life-Boat: Journal of the National Life-Boat Institution*, July 1st 1857, pages 72-76

18. Spratt H.P., *Merchant Steamers and Motorships, a Handbook of the Collections*, Science Museum, London, 1949

19. Lubbock B., *The China Clippers*, Brown, Son & Ferguson, Glasgow, 7th edition, 1929

20. Berthon E.L., *Collapsing Boats. Journal of the Royal United Services Institution*, 1877, pages 260 – 271. Paper presented Monday 1st May 1876

21. British Patent No. 5934, 1886

22. *The Times*, Wed., 1st November 1899

23. Scott J.D., *Siemens Brothers 1858–1958*, Weidenfeld & Nicholson, London, 1958

24. Jens, D., *The Berthon Story*, Classic Boat, No 82, April 1995, pages 42 – 48

25. *The Berthon Boat Company Ltd, Romsey; A Descriptive Account of Southampton* – Illustrated. Robinson Son & Co., Brighton, pages 33 – 36, undated

26. Nicholson Captain H.W., *The 700 mile Voyage in the Open Collapsible Canvas Boat*, The Union Jack Magazine, New Series, Volume 1; No. 12, 1882, Part I, Dec 19th pages 188 – 189; Part II, Dec 26th, pages 197 – 199

27. Berthon Boat Company Ltd, Romsey, *Catalogue and Price List*, undated but probably around 1902

28. Edwardes-Moss J., *A Season in Sutherland, 1889*, Quoted in Hastings Max, *Outside Days*, Michael Joseph Ltd., 1995

29. Lyon David, *The First Destroyers*, Chapman Publishing, London, 1996

30. *The Romsey Advertiser,* 25th October 2002, 'One Hundred Years Ago'.

31 Archives MNATP, *Collection Meillasoux*, Paris, http://www.culture./culture/atp/cdrom/francais/agh6.htm

32. Thomas P.N., *"P" Class Patrol Vessels*, The Model Shipwright, March 1979

33. Cody, S.F., *English Channel Crossing*, http.//mysite.freeserve.com/cody/english1.htm

34. Thomas R., *Before Britannia, A Photographic Archive of Family Yachts at Brodsworth Hall*, English Heritage Collections Review, 1999, pages 129 – 133

35. *The Berthon Folding Canoe*, The Engineer, May 1879, page 333

36. Hahn R., *The Engelhardt Collapsible*, Titanic Research and Modelling Association. http.//titanic-model.com/db/db-01/db_02.html

37. Heckstall-Smith B. and Hope L. ed., *A Manual of Yacht and Boat Sailing and Yacht Architecture*, Horace Cox, London, 11th edition 1913, pages 667 – 669

38. Zeni D., *The Forgotten Empress, The Empress of Ireland Story*, Halsgrove, Tiverton, Devon, 1998

39. Ovenden J. and Shayer D., *The Wreck of the Stella*, Guernsey Museums and Galleries, St Peter Port, 1999

40. Gardner R. and van der Vat D., *The Riddle of the Titanic*, Wiedenfeld & Nicholson, London, 1995

41. *Hampshire Advertiser*, April 27th 1912 and May 4th 1912

42. *Hampshire Independent*, April 27th 1912, May 4th 1912 and May 11th 1912

43. *The Romsey Advertiser*, 14th March 2003, One Hundred Years Ago

44. Hamilton F.T., *The Berthon Boat Company, Romsey*, Bournemouth Graphic, March 15th 1906, pages 170 - 173

View from Romsey Abbey Tower c1860
showing the triangular Market Place
and surrounding buildings
from the Slater Collection, courtesy of
King John's House & Tudor Cottage Trust (Romsey Heritage Centre)

SPECIAL NOTE
Cllr Slater was a chemist in Victorian Romsey. In 1858, his assistant, Mr Frost, introduced him to the new hobby of photography, which they soon put on a commercial basis. The photographs were taken for stereoscopic viewing, and covered a range of subject matter from portraits to views of Broadlands. Some of these photographs have survived, and give the earliest known photographic views of Romsey. The rear of the Slater shop is in the centre foreground of the view from the Abbey tower shown above.

ROMSEY IN BERTHON'S TIME

Barbara Burbridge

When the Rev. Berthon became vicar of Romsey in 1860, he came to a town of mixed fortunes. By the time of his death, in 1899, he had seen many fluctuations in the town's situation but only minor rises and falls in population.

A contemporary view comes from an old trade directory of 1859, the year before Berthon's arrival. Romsey was then described as 'a market and union town, railway and corporate borough'. The market referred to had existed from medieval times; the status of borough since 1607; but its perceived importance as the centre of a union of local workhouses and as a railway town was of much more recent date, and of more doubtful significance from the modern point of view.

Victorian Romsey was a small town, even though it had grown during the late-18th and early-19th century. A population of under 2000 in Tudor times had become 4000 by 1800 and 5500 by about 1830. These numbers, incidentally, included the scattered folk of rural Romsey Extra as well as those crowding the urban centre. Despite the influx of people between the 1750s and 1830s, the medieval framework of streets was not greatly enlarged. Rather, the rising numbers were accommodated through infilling.

The increase in population had been partly due to comparatively improved health and to a resulting decline in the death rate. It also reflected numerous incomers, drawn to the work opportunities offered by the town's success as a centre for the coach trade. As the new turnpike trusts developed from the mid-1700s onwards, Romsey was at the hub of roads to Winchester, Southampton, Salisbury, Ringwood and Stockbridge. All through-traffic had to cross Middlebridge on the south-west of town and traverse the Market Place itself.

But, having risen dramatically on the tide of a successful coaching trade and other prospering industries, such as papermaking, Romsey's population then remained more or less static throughout Berthon's time. Indeed, the population

59

actually dipped slightly for a while, at a time when many much smaller places were booming. The success that came to some communities with the railway age - and transformed places like Birmingham into great conurbations - passed Romsey by.

State of the Economy

Economically, Romsey was in the doldrums when the Rev. Berthon arrived, and had been for some time. The agricultural upheaval that had followed the enclosures at the beginning of the century had brought affluence to the fortunate ones who were now running larger but fewer farms. But it had left the small tenant farmers of old – the husbandmen – drifting as landless labourers.

The end of the Napoleonic wars had brought economic challenges. New mechanised techniques of paper manufacture, for example, were introduced from France, and left Romsey's paper mills unable to compete. Some millowners went bankrupt; others were forced to turn to making less profitable wrapping paper.

And the railway had brought much business failure in its wake. It may have kept the weekly cattle market buoyant, but it destroyed the old service economy based on the coaching trade. The first rail link from Bishopstoke to Salisbury had opened in 1847. Romsey station was located beyond the old town fields away from the edge of the built up area as it then was. There was little incentive for through travellers to make the effort of walking into the town.

Berthon would have seen the Andover to Southampton line open shortly after his arrival. It was largely built over the late-18th-century canal that had flowed southwards to the east of town. This second rail link was the coup-de-grace for coaching. The Bell Inn, once so significant that it had given its name to Bell Street, closed soon afterwards.

New Buildings

There had been a demand for cheap housing to accommodate the surge in population during the boom years of the early 1800s. As a result, Romsey was dotted with overcrowded areas such as the Banning Street alleys and courts that infilled one-time substantial plots. Many dwellings were poorly built and often too small to allow for the inclusion of basic amenities as and when they became available. Hygiene was impossible.

ex-Boys National School (now the public library) 1969

In contrast, from the 1830s onwards, the local authorities and the town's elite had enthusiastically adopted a widespread fashion for public building. Schools featured strongly. The presence in town of dissenting churches – notably Baptists, Congregationalists and Methodists – meant that two strands of sponsored schooling made education accessible to a wide range of children. The Church of England sponsored *The National Society* schools and the Nonconformists in their turn sponsored *The British & Foreign Bible Society* school. By 1835, the first National School for boys had appeared in Middlebridge Street as a result of Lord Palmerston's wish to remove the boys from their schoolroom within Romsey Abbey. By 1847, the elegant façade of the British School (now English Court, Winchester Road) had welcomed both boys and girls. A few years later, a National School for girls opened in Church Lane; now called Romsey Abbey Primary School, it is Romsey's oldest school building still serving its original function. In 1872, a new National School for boys (now the public library) replaced the earlier one of 1835.

The Union Workhouse that had become the centre for Romsey and district in the 1830s at first provided its own schoolroom, though the children later attended the British School. Additionally, three substantial charities specifically sponsored education of the poor. The St Barbe Charity of 1723 and the 19th-century Nowes Charity supported boys, while Lord Palmerston's mother had started a School of Industry for girls. Small older charities were amalgamated to provide for the poor generally. Almshouses were built or rebuilt to sustain a handful of carefully selected old women.

This was not the full extent of 19th-century public building. During the 1840s and 1850s, the townspeople must have been intrigued by the new-fangled police station close to the British School, and impressed by a new vicarage – the first purpose-built one in the town. This became home for the Rev. Berthon when he arrived in 1860.

Romsey Town Hall c1987
The Town Hall was opened in 1866. The statue of Lord Palmerston, who died in 1865, was erected in 1868

In the years immediately following, he must have watched the building of the Corn Exchange at the east end of the Market Place and the present Town Hall on its south side. Both the Methodists and the Congregationalists built new churches during the 1880s.

Banning Street in the 1950s, shortly before demolition
The crowded courts and alleys were off this street

The visual result of this uneven duality of development was a town where the centre gave an aura of modernity with impressive new civic buildings, but where the poor were living in overcrowded and unhygienic courts and alleys with increasingly dubious reputations.

Although saved by its small size to some extent, Romsey still suffered the new diseases of the 19th century. John Denner Blake, a shoemaker writing a diary in the late 1840s and early 1850s, recorded a fearful outbreak of cholera and the thanksgiving service in the Abbey when all seemed safe again. He also noted death from an older enemy, smallpox. Diseases such as these presented ongoing threats – together with others such as diphtheria, scarlet fever and tuberculosis that persisted as serious problems well into the 20th century.

At least the town was obliged to comply with Parliamentary decree in one respect, and 1857 saw the opening of a new cemetery in Botley Road on the eastern edge of town. It replaced the overcrowded churchyard, which had certainly become a health hazard. It also provided a Nonconformist as well as a Church of England chapel. This development was still not sufficient to stop the urgings of Lord Palmerston of Broadlands, who, until his death in 1865, frequently exhorted the corporation to improve the town's overall hygiene to save the people from typhus and cholera.

**Some of the Berthon Boatworks employees
with children
Mr Biddlecombe is the central figure with beard**

MR CLEMENT BIDDLECOMBE
GENERAL MANAGER OF THE BERTHON BOATBUILDING WORKS

*Richard Whiting has written the following, based on recollections
in his family records.*

Clement Biddlecombe was the General Manager of the Berthon
Boatbuilding works at Romsey. [He probably met his wife,
Elizabeth,] through her brother, Henry Holland Whiting, who was
living in Romsey. They lived in Portersbridge Street, Romsey,
and had a country retreat 'Squab Cottage', Squab Wood,
Romsey, originally an old coaching inn sometime known as the
'Ham and Cleaver'.

[Berthon] employed 100 workmen under Clement Biddlecombe
at the Romsey works, where they also built portable canvas
bandstands and a portable folding field hospital 20 feet in
diameter, holding five beds, which could be erected on the
battlefield and ready for use in 40 minutes.

The Rev. Berthon and Lord Palmerston had a sound appreciation of each other, even though they only overlapped for about five years. Undoubtedly, Lord Palmerston would have been impressed by Berthon's engineering enterprise, which was later to offer Romsey its first real economic life-line – though whether this was Berthon's intention, or simply a happy spin-off from his engineering enthusiasm, is another matter.

In a population of some 5,500 the potential male workforce would probably have been no more than 1500-2000. So when, with his son Edward Pearson Berthon as manager, the vicar expanded his boatworks in the late 1870s, and required about 100 people to work for him, this was hugely important for the town. The major product of collapsible boats had many applications, as is explained elsewhere in this book. They went to many assorted destinations both within this country and much further afield. It was significant, too, that these products from the boatworks left Romsey by rail; at long last Romsey was gaining a really positive advantage from the railway network.

Some ten years later, and there was an even greater reliance on rail transport. And the town had even more reason to be grateful to entrepreneur David Faber, a member of the publishing family. He, too, was determined to use the railway to advantage, this time for moving beer. There had only been small breweries to serve a limited hinterland, for beer did not travel well on those early roads; even the turnpikes were uneven and liable to render the brew undrinkable. But David Faber realised that the smoother transport offered by railways could be turned to business advantage. He bought up several small breweries, amalgamated them under the splendidly marketable name of Strong & Co. Ltd, and set up an enterprise that underpinned Romsey's economy for almost 100 years.

These two core industries of brewing and boatmaking gave extra stimulus to Romsey's existing economic mainstays based on tanyards, corn mills and paper mills - tanning and milling having been part of the economic framework from medieval times onwards. The confidence in Romsey shown by the Rev. Berthon and David Faber may have been inspired by the town's own improving self image. This was reflected in the extension of the borough of Romsey Infra in 1876, when the boundary between

Romsey Infra and Romsey Extra moved eastwards from its historic line along the Holbrook stream.

During the Victorian period, it is interesting to note the way in which Romsey was evolving socially. The market was a meeting point as well as a business centre, and the fairs three times a year (Easter Monday, 26th August and 8th November) were well supported, with stallholders for the cheese fair coming from as far afield as Somerset. The select band of successful farmers introduced an annual show, which ended in a splendid celebratory dinner. A Temperance Hall built in 1843 may have been an attempt to counterbalance such self-indulgence as well as constrain the excesses of the under-privileged.

Early on there were musical events for the better-off in the assembly rooms; supper evenings with singing and poetry recitals in rooms hired at the local hostelries; self-improvement at reading rooms and so on. The Reading Society in Romsey boasted over 1000 volumes. Chignell's, the stationer, had a 'news room'.

At the same time, people put up with hardships that are still part of living memory. Many will remember waking up on a cold winter's morning to the fascination of frost patterns on the windows. That keen diary writer, John Denner Blake, wrote of even harsher conditions prevailing in 19th-century Romsey. He recorded morning arrivals at his place of work with Mr Chollocombe, the Market Place shoemaker, and having to break the ice in the bowl of water before he could start his day.

In the Abbey, the congregation shivered. How Berthon contributed towards solving that problem is part of a separate chapter.

~~~~~~~~~~~~~~~~~~~~~~~~~~~~~

Sources
Hampshire Record Office
LTVAS publications (listed inside front cover)
LTVAS Archives

A Berthon Boat for the 'Viking Invaders', 1907

BERTHON 'LONGSHIPS'
A Different Sort of Challenge

In 1907, Romsey marked the traditional foundation of Romsey Abbey a thousand years before. An area along the River Test in Broadlands Park was the setting for a grand millenary pageant depicting major events in the history of Romsey and its Abbey. The third episode in this stirring representation was entitled *The Destruction of Romsey Abbey by the Danes, AD994.*

The LTVAS publication *A Slice of Old Romsey* (1975) records:

The Danish ships, which actually sailed up the river during the pageant, were constructed 'by skilled mechanics of the Berthon Collapsible Boat Works in the Town'.

67

**The Interior of Romsey Abbey, c1836
showing the 18th-century west gallery
with the Coster organ of 1782 backed by a huge curtain**

Romsey Abbey: the Berthon Years, 1860-1892

Francis J. Green

North Side of Romsey Abbey c1860
as the Rev. Berthon would have seen it on his arrival in Romsey
Drawing by Judd, published by Lordan of Romsey

The year 907AD is the traditional date for the founding of Romsey Abbey as a community of nuns, though the documented evidence only starts with King Edgar's 967AD foundation as a Benedictine nunnery. The present Abbey church, built on the site of at least two earlier smaller churches, dates from the 12th and early-13th centuries, taking some 130 years to complete. The impressive Romanesque and early gothic building suffered many alterations over the following centuries. Five years after Henry VIII dissolved the nunnery in 1539, the town purchased the building as its parish church. Later changes related to its new function and to liturgical needs over succeeding centuries.

Thus the changes introduced through the Reformation and the Puritanical zeal of the Civil War period destroyed much that had been treasured from earlier times. The lengthy sermons and readings of 18th-century Anglicanism led to the introduction of galleries for the congregation in the nave and both north and

69

south transepts. John Bullar, writing in 1819, says 'the general effect of the interior of the church is utterly ruined by the pews and galleries with which the central part is fitted up for worship'.

As with many major ecclesiastical buildings, particularly those with strong civic connections, the later significant 'improvements' were undertaken to provide for the greater comfort of the congregation and their closer proximity to the preacher. These alterations not only reflected the changing nature of worship and liturgical ideals but also musical provision.

Additional windows were inserted in some parts of the church, notably through the west walls of the Romanesque blind arcading of the transepts. This provided additional light to the early 18th-century galleries there. The lowering of the roof above the north and south transept apses allowed windows to be inserted directly into the open arches of the triforium. The Abbess's doorway in the south aisle was partially blocked with masonry and contained a wooden frame with lead lights. This is illustrated in the third edition of Charles Spence's work, *An Essay Descriptive of the Abbey Church of Romsey* (1851) and was probably constructed in the mid-18th century.

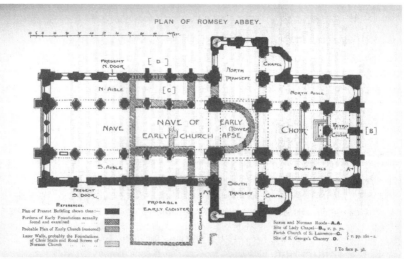

Plan of Romsey Abbey, as presented in Edwardian times
from Henry Liveing's Records of Romsey Abbey, published in 1906

70

The 19th century began with the continuation of the Georgian aim of achieving creature comforts for the congregation. Earlier fabric was destroyed in 1823-4, when the church was given new box-pews, and the arcades of the chancel were infilled to create a draught-free area.

Corporation Box-Pew, Romsey Abbey
Drawing made before the removal of box-pews
showing blocked arches in background

Many of the old fittings and fixtures were swept away. Fortunately, information about these survive in unpublished form, notably in the writings and drawings of Dr John Latham (1740-1837), whose seven volumes about Romsey are held by the British Library, and in the work of early 19th-century artists such as Cattermole and Buckler.

Other momentous changes also took place in the land around the Abbey in the decades before Berthon's arrival. Some forty years earlier, the parish had regained the south side of the 24-foot walkway that had been included in the purchase of the church from Henry VIII in 1544, but which had long since been alienated. Rather than using this area for its designated purpose, the parish officers made it part of the churchyard and took full opportunity to sell grave spaces. It rapidly became cluttered with monuments and burials.

South-east corner of Romsey Abbey c1860
from Slater Collection, courtesy of King John's House & Tudor Cottage Trust
(Romsey Heritage Centre)

Evidence revealed by archaeological excavations between 1974 and 1991 demonstrated the damage caused by the insertion of vaults and brick-lined graves from 1820 until 1857, when the

72

new town cemetery opened. By then, the grave-digging had resulted in the loss of significant archaeological deposits from the 7th century onwards. Many of the vaults close to the walls of the church had even compromised the footings of the Romanesque building. This early 19th-century layout of the churchyard was, indeed, only changed in the 20th century, well after Berthon's time.

Changes to the fabric of the church itself continued in the 19th century. The space beneath the central crossing tower contained virtually nothing of the pre-1539 monastic choir arrangements. The medieval walls that separated the retro-choir from the choir aisles did survive, although they would not escape Berthon's attention in the years to come. The misericord choir seats and the remaining fragments of parclose screen, recorded by Dr John Latham in the early 1800s had mostly been discarded and the only surviving pieces stored in roof spaces.

Similarly, portions of medieval painted glass had been removed. Fortunately, these were recorded in drawings by Dr John Latham between 1808 and 1816 and further described by the Revd John Louis Pettit in 1846.

Many areas of medieval encaustic floor tile had already been destroyed to make way for family burial vaults beneath the floor. Other brick-vaulted aboveground tombs had been constructed in the south aisle and in the retro-choir. These were removed in the 1840s when the interior was partially repaved with York stone. Many medieval floor tiles were salvaged and recorded at this time. Those that survived this process can still be viewed in the apse floor of St George's chapel and on the internal step of the Abbess's doorway.

The details of the early 19th-century internal arrangements of the church are well illustrated in the view, c1836, from Moody's *History of Hampshire*, reproduced on page 276 of Liveing's *Records of Romsey Abbey*. The engraving shows the west gallery with the 1782 organ built by Coster of Salisbury. The organ was backed by a huge curtain that rose from the gallery to the apex of the surviving medieval nave roof. It was variously described as red, scarlet or pink, no doubt the colour change reflecting fading of the fabric over time.

As the Victorian era began, some began to look critically at the whole interior of the Abbey church, not only the way it had become cluttered with galleries but also the extensive lime-washing that had been regularly applied throughout the post-reformation period. Contemporary accounts likened it to the interior of a chalk pit, a description provided by the sexton, William Major, in his manuscript notes. Major was allowed to start the process of scraping away the limewash in the 1840s, and revealing the nearly invisible stonework carvings in their original crisp detail.

SW View of Nave
Published by Lordan of Romsey

The interior of the nave in 1860 is best illustrated by the lithographs published by Charles Lordan of Romsey and used in the fourth edition of Spence's *Essay* in 1862. One shows the nave looking west. The large lithographic view of the 1850s, also published by Lordan, shows the nave looking eastwards. Berthon was in some ways fortunate that the process of returning the interior of the Abbey from a huge preaching barn, more like the auditorium of a theatre than the building seen today, was started in 1844. This work, under the auspices of the Hon. Gerard Noel, Vicar of Romsey 1841-51, involved raising and expending the not inconsiderable sum of £2,000 between 1841 and 1849. Benjamin Ferry (1810-1880), the noted gothic revival architect and pupil of A.C. Pugin, was chosen to design and supervise restoration and repair work.

The process of renovation and reorganisation, particularly within the nave of the church, had therefore mostly been completed before 1860. It had involved the removal of the west gallery and organ, allowing the entirety of the nave to be viewed from east to west for the first time in over a hundred years. After the Rev. Noel's death, the work continued through the 1850s when the Rev. C. Avery Moore was vicar. A new nave roof was constructed to Ferry's design costing £2,000; the money was raised through a voluntary rate. Indeed, most of the alterations prior to 1868 were funded through voluntary rather than imposed church rates.

Ferry also carefully conserved the stonework of the great west window, and provided designs for the adjacent former vicarage (now Folly House) and Romsey Abbey School. A new organ manufactured by Walker was placed on the north transept gallery in 1857.

Berthon Continues the Work

Berthon's first major work of repair was to the roof of the north transept. The new roof was also designed by Ferry; constructed by George Wheeler of Romsey, it has a span of 34 feet. Berthon contributed his knowledge of boat building techniques for its construction. Work involved bending 12 one-inch thick wooden planks, which were laminated and riveted together to produce the large curving timber ribs. This method of construction, as used at Romsey, is not unique and there are other examples associated with boat builders. A similar principle of construction was used at St Peter's church on the Isle of Dogs in the London dockland in 1859-1860. Not satisfied with helping to design the roof, Berthon records that he then actually carved and gilded the roof bosses and the decorative detail on the cornices. It is doubtful if any of Berthon's predecessors could claim such a close practical involvement in changes that took place during their incumbencies.

Berthon could not resist commenting that the north transept roof cost under half that of the chancel, which was replaced less than a year later. The chancel roof, spanning an identical space, was, however, built of oak. The roof was designed by Ewen Christian (1814-1895), the architect of the Ecclesiastical

Commissioners. The Commissioners were in part legally responsible for repairs and maintenance of the chancel. Ewen Christian is noted for his work on other major churches, such as Southwell Minster.

Berthon, on page 158 of his memoirs, noted that nothing had been done to the furnishings in the chancel and 'that high backed pews with curtains round' remained, including that of the late Lord Palmerston. Undoubtedly, the present appearance of the chancel, with views to the eastern windows within the ambulatory, is entirely due to Berthon's and Ewen Christian's work. They considered that the building's appearance would be better served by the removal of the retro-choir walls, and this was duly recorded in the local paper, *The Romsey Register, on* 10th January and 11th July 1867. Following on from his comments about old pews, Berthon recorded that 'an antiquated Cambridge Don remonstrated with me for opening the lower arches, averring that I should make the chancel *look like a four-post bedstead'.*

The work involved further problems for Berthon to solve. New encaustic tiles, laid on the chancel floor in the 1840s, were set in a hard cement and could not be individually taken up and relaid. It would have cost £140 to replace them completely, so, in order to accommodate the re-organisation proposed by himself and Christian, Berthon applied his practical skills. He simply had workmen undermine sections of the tiles complete with their concrete backing, the sections being numbered so that they could be refitted. He further recorded that this cost only 38 shillings.

This preparatory work ultimately allowed the 1857 Walker organ console to be removed in 1887-8 from the gallery in the north transept. It was then possible to re-organise the choir along the lines of the Oxford Movement. The re-introduction of ceremonial and ritual into Anglican worship focused on the sacrament of communion. This involved the move away from the lengthy homilies and sermons and the extensive readings of biblical text that had characterised worship from the 17th century onwards. Berthon managed to relocate the choir, moving it from the north gallery into the chancel next to the organ. Later, in 1870, he introduced the wearing of surplices, some thirty years after members of the Oxford Movement first restarted this tradition.

Clearly, the whole re-organisation of the church interior, but particularly the chancel at Romsey, has to be viewed in this context. Also, it should not be forgotten that John Keble, one of the Oxford Movement's principle proponents, was vicar of the nearby parish of Hursley until his death in 1862. He may have even directly influenced Berthon. However, Berthon's own churchmanship cannot be ignored. In a seven-page Christmas letter to his congregation in 1867 Berthon outlined his view that he was fully committed to the principles of the Reformation. He said 'that he would ever guard against any introductions that even seem to be opposed to those principles; but on the other hand would wish to avoid the slovenly and unauthorized methods of conducting divine service which had crept into our churches generally'.

By 1868, Berthon had already achieved much and had been supported in his work until 1865 by Lord Palmerston, who was not generally noted for liking the clergy. Berthon and Lord Palmerston collaborated, for esample on improving the heating in the Abbey by organising the installation of Gurney stoves. These stoves survived long into the 20th century.

A Gurney Stove
one of those installed in the 1860s after Berthon's arrival as Vicar of Romsey

Lord Palmerston's heir and successor was the Hon. William Cowper-Temple; in contrast to Palmerston, he was noted for holding open-air prayer meetings at Broadlands. William helped significantly to finance and promote further repairs and embellishments to the church.

Berthon himself records that so much needed to be done, noting that 'there were no choir stalls, even when the organ greatly improved was brought down; there was no screen, no chancel step, and as for the pulpit, it was so horrible that on two separate occasions I had it cut down, destroying the reading desk and clerk's pew'. As Berthon records on page 165 of his *Retrospect*, it was finally replaced in oak with the figures of the evangelists being carved by Harry Hems of Exeter but the rest by Wheeler's of Romsey. A good description of some of Berthon's work is contained in the Hampshire Chronicle for 17th November 1888, reporting on the great service of re-dedication at which the Bishop of Winchester preached. It states that 'the case for the enlarged organ was designed by the vicar out of the old one'.

Inside & Out
With the removal of the retro-choir walls, the lower pair of the eastern windows came into full view. Berthon describes the dismay of Ewen Christian, the architect, at the clumsy way these windows had been jammed into place so that parts of the heads had been lost. This had happened in the post-Reformation period when 13th-century eastern chapels had been demolished and their window tracery and jambs salvaged and re-used in the blocking of the arcade between the retro-choir and the former chapels. Early photographs of the 1860s show the awkward arrangement to which Berthon refers. The Ecclesiastical Commissioners refused to provide a grant in 1866 to make new windows on the grounds of expense, and Berthon was yet again forced to use his ingenuity to produce the aesthetically satisfactory appearance seen today.

On page 159 of his *Retrospect*, Berthon explains in great detail the process of solving the problem of the east windows. It involved severing the window jambs from the surrounding masonry and cutting away stonework below the windows to allow them to be lowered on screw jacks, glass and all. It took three hours to lower each window into its present position. The masonry jambs were re-secured and the vertical joints that are proof of this work can still be seen. The missing heads of the windows were replaced in new stonework. Recent stone-cleaning has revealed that the Victorian stonework was toned down to match older masonry by using mat black paint. This can still be seen even after the stone-cleaning of 1996.

East End of Romsey Abbey c1860
Showing the uneven state of the lower east windows
before restoration by the Rev. Berthon

Again in the chancel area Berthon was responsible for the construction of the wooden screen that now separates the north transept and the choir. The screen, a memorial to his wife who died in 1865 a few months before Lord Palmerston, was designed by an architect called Purday. In Berthon's time, the screen was placed on the chancel step on the east side of the crossing. The cresting and carved frieze of heads within trefoils were re-used from fragments of the medieval screen that Berthon had located in one of the roof spaces in 1860, and which had previously been recorded *in situ* by Latham.

The replacement of the glass in the great west window as a memorial to Lord Palmerston was undertaken by the firm of Clayton and Bell at a cost of £1,200. It was not generally considered an artistic, or for that matter a suitable, addition to the church. Berthon clearly expressed his views about its lack of merit. The window was removed in the early 1960s. The description of Berthon's pyrotechnic lighting of this window at its inauguration, was inspired he says by night-time illumination of the windows that he had seen at St Peter's in Rome.

79

Berthon had the support of many local gentry and landowners in his work on the Abbey. However, it must not be forgotten that he met with stiff resistance from some parishioners. In part, this was probably due to trying to introduce changes too soon after those made by the Rev. Noel.

Equally, there was resistance to his view that private pews and their rents were abominable. Although the box-style pews in the nave had been replaced, the new pews were still private and lockable and did not provide any flexibility for arranging the seating. There was no central aisle or access between the pews in the eastern part of the nave until they were finally replaced by rush-seated 'cathedral' chairs in 1888. A circular dated 6th January 1887 reveals that the works undertaken at that time resulted from the fund raising appeal for £1,600 as a local memorial for the 50th year of the reign of Queen Victoria.

Berthon was clearly interested in the architecture, history and archaeology of the Abbey church. It is therefore surprising, given this appreciation, that few tangible illustrative records survive. It would appear that, with all his scientific knowledge and inventions, he was not an avid photographer. For example, amongst the photographs of the Abbey that survive from this period, there are currently no known views of the 1857 Walker organ on the north transept gallery before it was moved. There are only odd oblique views, such as the one published in *The Illustrated London News* for November 1865 in relation to the then recent death of Lord Palmerston.

Similarly, the form of the original roofs over the north transept and the chancel were seemingly not recorded before they were removed. If any detailed records were ever made they have not been located. Various engravings and line illustrations from the early 19th century onwards show the timber and painted canvas chancel ceiling. The ceiling, probably dating from the 16th century, was certainly decorated with angels and the Romsey portcullis heraldic symbol. It is unfortunate that no portion of the ceiling has survived, even though some panels were retained at the time.

**Interior of Romsey Abbey, looking east
as it would have looked when Berthon first arrived**
This drawing shows the new nave roof
with the old chancel ceiling just visible beyond the crossing
Published by Lordan of Romsey

The generally careful observation and conservation during Berthon's time can be seen in the surviving painted decoration on the piers, just below capital level either side of the treasury cabinet between the south aisle and the choir. These areas of wall painting had been concealed by the construction of the retro-choir wall in the late 13th[th] or early 14th century. The *Romsey Register* of 3rd October 1867 records the removal of the wall in that year. It had separated the eastern portion of the choir from the choir aisles and rose in height to within a few inches of the capitals of the piers.

Elsewhere in the Abbey church, Berthon and those involved with the work of restoration very deliberately retained portions of medieval wall paintings, which had clearly not been stripped by the over-thorough scraping and cleaning of the interior in the 1840s and 1850s.

Berthon records that the original north transept roof, the gable of which had survived to full height, had involved the re-use of the original timbers at a lower pitch. These timbers retained portions of original colour and mouldings thought at that time to be of late 15th-century date. It is quite probable that the north transept roof may have actually been replaced in the early 16th century along with the roof of the central crossing tower.

Apart from the renovation and alterations to the buildings fabric, with which he was personally involved, Berthon clearly appreciated the archaeological importance of many items and realised that the renovation work of the 1840s had resulted in many significant losses, such as the 13th-century font. He specifically comments on the use of stonework that did not match original materials in colour or in the method of tooling their surfaces, and in many places consisted only of painted plaster. However, the fact that these repairs can still be seen today, although not harmonious, tell their own story.

Berthon also recalls the finding of the cresset lamps, discovered in the masonry built against the pier arcade of the first bay on the south side of the choir when it was unblocked. He wrote a letter on this subject to the Romsey Register of 1st October 1867.

Medieval Window, as rebuilt in the old vicarage garden

Berthon's illicit night-time excavations to the east of the church, outside the churchyard, provided details of the length of the eastern chapels, demolished at the dissolution. Having left no drawn or photographic record, it has never been possible to verify his statements fully. The stonework salvaged from the various renovation and restoration projects within the church has survived. Berthon was responsible for erecting these fragments as a garden feature or folly in his own vicarage garden (now Folly House). The fragments, including complete window tracery from the replaced north aisle windows, testify to the accuracy of early 19th-century prints and drawings.

The folly provides an invaluable repository of historic Abbey stonework. It also acts as a reminder that Berthon was responsible for the reproduction Romanesque windows in the eastern bays of the north aisle, clearly a well-informed restoration but not good conservation. This point is noted by Berthon himself in a letter to Spence, as reported in Spence's notebook, page 196. These windows were substituted for the battered perpendicular ones that had originally been inserted beneath the arcade of the additional north aisle, when the parish church was no longer restricted to that aisle after the dissolution.

Berthon's own large watercolour reconstruction view of the nunnery church from the south-east also survives. This is to be found outside the choir vestry in the north choir aisle. It demonstrates the extent of his archaeological knowledge and interpretation of the cloister and church building.

Berthon's own words in 1889, quoted by Luce, express his satisfaction: 'it is a joy to see our church advancing gradually to

83

its original beauty, now showing since the removal of the galleries, [and] the destruction of the pews'.

Berthon was undoubtedly a man of strong views and vision. In a period of some 30 years, he managed to undertake a major re-ordering of the interior of the Abbey church. He achieved an interior that was better suited to the changing patterns of worship and liturgy and more in keeping with the character of this former great Benedictine nunnery church.

The Abbess's Doorway, c1851 partially blocked and converted into a window (since restored as a doorway)
as depicted in Charles Spence's essay on Romsey Abbey

Berthon's re-ordering forms the basis of the Abbey church today, although no longer quite as he left it. His quire screen, for example, has been repositioned to give totally uninterrupted internal views from the west and east ends of this great Romanesque church. Overall, however, Berthon made a major contribution to the way the building can be used for its primary purpose of worship today, and his portrait is to be found in the Berthon memorial window in the north transept.

One of Berthon's unfulfilled ambitions for the Abbey was the creation of a new north porch, the medieval one having been demolished in the early 15th century to make way for an extension that was itself demolished after the dissolution. This porch was eventually constructed to the design of William Caroe (1857-1938), the funds coming from the proceeds of the 1907 Romsey millenary celebrations. In a very real sense, Berthon's spirit, like his boats, lived on into the 20th century.

84

Bibliography

Berthon, E.L., *A Retrospect of Eight Decades* George Bell & Sons, London, 1899

Britton J., *A chronological History and Graphic Illustrations of Christian Architecture in England*, London, Longman, Rees, Orme, Brown and Green, 1827

Cook-Yarborough, J., *The Ancient Abbey Church of Saint Mary and Saint Ethelflaeda at Romsey an Appeal for funds to save it from decay*. Leaflet and covering letter, May 1896; account of expenditure, 1899

Green, F.J., *The Bell Frames and Belfry at Romsey Abbey*, In Brooke C.J. (ed) The Archaeology of Bellframes, Nottinghamshire County Council, 1996

Latham, J., *Unpublished History of Romsey*, British Library, BL Mss 26774-26780

Liveing, H.G.D.,1906 *Records of Romsey Abbey*, Warren and Son, Winchester,

Pevsner, N., *Hampshire and the Isle of Wight, The Buildings of England*, Penguin, Harmondsworth, 1967

Ridley, J., *Lord Palmerston*, Book Club Associates, London, 1970

Russel, A.D., *The report on the medieval floor tiles from Romsey Abbey 122-142*, In Scott, I. R. (ed), Romsey Abbey Report on the Excavations 1973-1991. Hampshire Field Club and Archaeological Society, Monograph 8, Sutton, Stroud

Scott, I.R., *Romsey Abbey: Report on the Exacavations 1973-1991*, Hampshire Field Club and Archaeological Society, Monograph 8, Sutton, Stroud, 1996

Spence, C., *An Essay Descriptive of the Abbey Church of Romsey* (3rd ed.) Lordan, Romsey; Houlson and Stoneman, London, 1851

Spence, C., *An Essay Descriptive of the Abbey Church of Romsey* (4th ed.) Lordan, Romsey; Longman, London, 1862

Walker, F.G., (ed), *A short History of Romsey*, Chignell, Romsey, 1896

Sources

- 19th-century Parish Magazines
- Hampshire Record Office, Winchester
- Local Newspapers

- Lower Test Valley Archaeological Study Group records, *including transcriptions of many privately held manuscripts*
- Parish Office archives, *including notebooks of Charles Spence, essayist, and* William Major, 19th-century sexton
- Romsey Parochial Papers
- Southampton University Archives, *especially for the unpublished notes on 'Romsey Abbey since 1800' by Sir Richard Luce*

Acknowledgements

Thanks are particularly due to
- Canon Neil Crawford-Jones, Vicar of Romsey
- Hampshire Record Office staff
- LTVAS Group members
- Students who have provided copies of their essays and dissertations on various aspects of Romsey Abbey church
- Judy Walker, winner of the Local History Annual Writers Competition in 1998, for access to her essay entitled *The Transformation of the Interior of Romsey Abbey Church during one Vicar's Incumbency (The Rev. E. L. Berthon, Vicar 1860-1892)*

~~~~~~~~~~~~~~~~

Imaginative View of Romsey Abbey SE in 12th Century Painting by the Rev. E.L. Berthon, 1866
By permission of the Vicar of Romsey

86

UNDERLYING PRINCIPLES
Canon Neil Crawford-Jones, Vicar of Romsey

It may seem odd to begin an article about the Revd E. L. Berthon, my distinguished predecessor, by quoting at length from a journal begun by his immediate successor, the Revd Cooke-Yarborough. The journal begins on the day of Mr Cooke-Yarborough's institution as Vicar of the parish - 29th May 1892.

He begins:
"May 29th - I arrive by the night mail reaching my lodgings in the Abbey at 12.30. May 27th, my dear wife joining me on the following afternoon.
On Sunday 29th the retiring Vicar, the Revd. E. L. Berthon, celebrated at a Choral Celebration at 8am - linen vestments and candles lighted. Procession starting from the Chancel, cross, two banners. Service well rendered by the Choir. Mattins 11. Evensong at 6.30.

At 3pm about half a dozen clergy having assembled to meet the Bishop, he arrived, and the choir being drawn up at the south side of the church, he joined them from the Vicarage and the special service of Institution began.

The Bishop's address was deeply solemn and moving. God grant that I may have strength and power faithfully to minister in this great parish and noble church.

On Monday May 30th I commenced my duties by Mattins at 8.30 and gave directions that the services should be carried on as usual for the present. Meeting the Bishop at 10 at Romsey Station I travelled with him to Bishopstoke Junction to receive his counsel and advice on the following subjects:-
1)   retention of the Chalice
2)   reading the Gospel and Epistle with back to the people
3)   wearing of biretta.
He advised as I expected, or rather approved of my intention to abolish these.
4)   the use of the ante-communion service every Sunday after Mattins.

87

He approved, provided means were taken not to decrease the length of the sermon. Advised the Litany being said in the afternoon or evening.

5)   the checking of the Archbishop's judgement of November 1890 as a standard and limit of ritual approved.

6)   as to vestments I propose to discontinue the chasuble after telling him that I believed that the Prayer Book ordered its use.

The Bishop, speaking as a friendly advisor, pointed out the difficulty of re-introducing them in the event of my now discontinuing and advised that they should be allowed to stand if I felt them to be "vital". I replied that I did not consider them vital but that I was glad to concur with his advice.

The Bishop advised me if I took the Archbishop's judgement as my guide, to do so at once without waiting for the decision of the Parish Council. The Bishop advised me not to put any matter to the vote with my people. I am deeply thankful to Almighty God for making my way so clear as to these difficult points."

To a 21st century Vicar it seems extraordinary that a new Vicar should arrive in the parish and see his immediate predecessor fully in operation and command. Times certainly have changed. However, the point of this brief article re-visiting my two predecessors is to remember Mr Berthon not simply as an engineer, inventor, or mere beautifier of the Abbey Church. There were indeed important principles at work behind the very considerable re-arrangements that he achieved in the Abbey.

There are old photographs dating from the time before Mr Berthon's re-ordering and re-furnishing of the Abbey. They are taken from the gallery in the south transept looking over the crossing towards the north transept and its gallery.

There is no doubt that to modern eyes the interior of the place seems untidy and the arrangement of pews higgledy-piggledy and haphazard. The large two-decker pulpit in its old position against the north-east corner of the crossing gives some indication of the prominence given to the sermon and non-eucharistic services in the parish at that time. It would be wrong to attribute to Mr Berthon merely archaeological interests in taking out the galleries in the north and south transepts and removing the pews. We know what a controversial course of action this proved to be in the eyes of many of the parishioners. Mr Berthon certainly would have made the Abbey look much more as we might expect a Church of England parish to look.

His achievement must indeed have made the church look very different to parishioners as they came to worship. Not only were the pews gone from the nave, and galleries from the transepts, but a screen was erected across the eastern arch of the crossing, and the chancel beyond it was equipped with fine choir stalls and clergy stalls and a pew on the south side for the family of Lord Palmerston. The high altar was provided with dorsal curtains and eventually a very fine pulpit was installed in place of the two-decker pulpit.

Clearly, there were underlying principles to all this, including the re-positioning of the organ in 1888. This was carefully done to ensure that the view right down the length of the church in the north aisle was uninterrupted. The technology of organ building at the time was stretched virtually to its limit. But the organ was brought near to the robed choir in the chancel. Berthon was clearly influenced by the liturgical fashions and movements of his day. He would have achieved a dignified and worthy setting for worship offered in a fitting way in such a major building. His wearing of eucharistic vestments and birettas and the carrying of banners indicate that he was strongly influenced by the ritual fashions that arose out of the Oxford movement. It is a rather nice accident that a later carving showing Mr Berthon wearing his biretta is now to be seen on the Vicar's stall, as repositioned by Canon Corban, who was Vicar from 1929-1951.

The fact that Mr Cooke-Yarborough needed to raise questions on the train with the Bishop of Winchester about some of the ritual arrangements in Romsey Abbey will help us to understand that Mr Berthon was, in many respects, quite advanced for his day. He was what we might call a High Churchman. What I find interesting, however, is that given the reservations that Mr Cooke-Yarborough had with regard to certain practices in Romsey Abbey, he was nevertheless responsible for re-establishing the daily celebration of the Holy Communion in our parish church. This was a recovery of Catholic rather than merely High Church practice. The fact that it has continued since 1897 is an indication of the perception that successive Vicars of Romsey have had, both of their ministry and the place of the parish church within the community. We are here primarily to worship God and part of our service of the community is to pray for it on a regular basis.

I cannot but help to be fascinated by my predecessors and by what I have been able to discover about them. Let me end with three clergymen, not Berthon, as I share with the reader the fact that there is in the vestry of the church a photograph of three incumbents of Romsey. Cooke-Yarborough stands in a Victorian clerical frock coat holding what we might call a curé hat. One of his successors, Andrew Robertson, is shown in a hairy tweed suit. He came to Romsey to tone down the liturgical excesses of his predecessor Martin Tapper. Canon Corban is shown wearing a Church of England double-breasted cassock. The different modes of dress show something of the nature of these three men, of their different personalities but also of the fact that time and the Church have moved on. They continue to do so.

In 2004, we have reached a point where many of the chairs, surviving from the Berthon refurbishing, are finally giving up the ghost. Wear and tear and beetles are making them unreliable and unsafe.

Nonetheless, much of Berthon's achievement survives, built on and developed by those privileged to have followed him, surely one of the most memorable Vicars of Romsey.

Carving of Berthon's Head
Vicar's Stall in Romsey Abbey Choir

POSTSCRIPT & ANECDOTES

After the death of the Rev. Berthon, the boatworks continued to flourish for a further decade under the leadership of the vicar's son, Edward Pearson Berthon, who had always managed the boatyard for his father. The following accounts reveal how the boats continued to be of use long after the Romsey company had closed down.

The English Heritage *discovery of a Berthon boat generated several articles in newspapers and magazines, to which there was considerable response.*

PERSONAL MEMORY OF HANDLING A BERTHON BOAT
Captain Sir Thomas Barlow wrote to Country Life *magazine with a copy to* English Heritage. *He recalls that Berthon boats continued to be used by the navy until the mid-20th century.*

[The] boat was a standard item of equipment in submarines on the China Station before the Second War. We were never quite sure what we were supposed to do with it, but it may have been meant to help us get on board ships, which might have been attacked by pirates, a very serious problem in Chinese waters at that time. Mercifully, we never had to try. It was stowed outside the pressure hull of the submarine, in the casing, where it did not matter if it got wet when we submerged. It was an awkward creature to assemble, and it was not a speedy operation, nor was it very stable when you did get it into the water. Despite that, it was sometimes used for recreational purposes, and once, in the early months of 1940, it almost saw active service. I recall being landed on the beach of one of the islands in the Chagos Group in the Indian Ocean to find out from the owner of the local coconut plantation if he had sighted any suspicious ships, which might have been German commerce raiders. Eventually we left it in the dockyard in Malta, where it presumably ended up as a target for Italian bombers.

The Berthon boatyard with Abbey beyond
(Pre-World War II view looking westwards)

The long arched building in the left foreground was the main workshed of the Berthon Boat Company. The open yard may be seen to the right. There were other smaller buildings on the site.

A BERTHON BOAT, 'ex-WD'
STILL IN USE AFTER WORLD WAR 2

Mr A.V. Yearsley wrote to the Country Life *magazine to relate his memories about a folding boat, which by its description sounds very like one of Berthon design.*

The design [of Berthon folding boats] was used for the forces (which one I know not) in WWII as my father bought a 12-foot version in about 1947, 'ex-WD'. It was made of double-skinned canvas, folded flat and was very light and rigid when extended. He also bought an 'ex-WD' Seagull outboard which would propel it at remarkable speed flat out, the only problem being that the stern went down to such an extent that water started to get in between the canvas plies where there was a gap at the stern.

In later letters to English Heritage, *he added:*
I think that my father bought the boat and outboard from war surplus stores at Chatham, where there were both army engineer and Royal Navy establishments.

I seem to remember that the canvas was originally some sort of military dark green, so my father applied a couple of coats of light grey oil paint to brighten up the appearance, both inside and out. I do not think that we had any repair kit.

A BERTHON BOAT IN THE 1960s

Mr Richard Whiting, descendant of Clement Biddlecombe, also recalls a post-war use of a Berthon boat.

I do remember coming across a forbidding headmistress of a girls' school in Towyn struggling to put together a folding boat on the banks of a river in mid-Wales in (what must have been) 1968 who explained that her craft was a Berthon boat.

The Abbey Crossing looking NE, 1895
The Rev. Berthon is shown, wearing his biretta (right foreground).
This drawing was made some three years after his retirement.

One final thought

As the Rev. Berthon strolled around the Abbey church that he cared for so deeply, perhaps he occasionally paused beside the memorial effigy of Sir William Petty in the south-west corner of the nave, and contemplated the many similarities in their lives and interests – despite being separated by some two centuries.

Both had noble connections, though in reverse. Whilst Berthon was descended from a French marquis, Petty – born into trade but knighted by Charles II – is now the esteemed direct ancestor of the Marquess of Lansdowne. Similarly, their common link with Romsey was also of a contrasting nature, Petty being born and bred in the town but living his adult life in London or abroad, and Berthon arriving at the age of 47 to spend his remaining 39 years in the town.

Both men were polymaths. Both could draw, and used these skills in their design work – with Petty applying his talent additionally in the world of map-making. Both were involved in the medical world – Berthon through his training as a surgeon, Petty as professor of anatomy at Brasenose College, Oxford. Berthon's appreciation of Paganini's playing is matched by Petty's tenure as head of Gresham College of Music.

Incredibly, both were boat builders working from their own designs, each of which was remarkably original in its own way and time. While the 19th-century Berthon devised his folding boats, Sir William Petty, in the 17th century, successfully produced what must surely have been the first English twin-hulled boat. Jeff Hawksley of the LTVAS Group has made precision models of these innovative designs, and they are displayed in Romsey's Heritage Centre.

In the end each man contributed to the welfare of Romsey, Petty through an educational endowment, Berthon through the life-line that his boatworks offered to the economy of a very depressed little town.

No wonder the lives of these two men have been considered worthy of celebration. The tercentenary of Petty's death was marked in grand style in 1987. In the year 2004 it was time to appreciate fully the Reverend Edward Lyon Berthon.

ABOUT THE CONTRIBUTORS

Virginia Arrowsmith, BA, MA, AMA
Virginia Arrowsmith is an Assistant Regional Curator for English Heritage. Based in North Yorkshire, she covers the three North regions of English Heritage and specialises in social and oral history. Working with the Lower Test Valley Archaeological Study Group (LTVAS), she curated the exhibition 'Berthon's Collapsible Boats' at Brodsworth Hall in 2002.

Barbara Burbridge, BA
A long-time LTVAS committee member, Barbara Burbridge acts as the group's Vice-Chairman and Editor. She is also management chairman of King John's House & Tudor Cottage Trust, which runs Romsey Heritage Centre. Her particular interests are the economic development of Romsey and the study of Medieval Latin.

Canon Neil Crawford-Jones
Canon Neil Crawford-Jones became Vicar of Romsey in 1984 and was appointed Hon. Canon of Winchester in 1992.

Francis J. Green, BA, MPhil, MSc, MIFA, IHBC
Francis J. Green is Test Valley Borough Council's Heritage Officer, working within the Planning Service. He was previously (1980-97) director of the Test Valley Archaeological Trust. In both capacities he has been closely involved with Romsey Abbey, bringing specialist knowledge as a founder member of the Society for Church Archaeology. His other specialisms are environmental archaeology and buildings conservation.

Jeff Hawksley, BSc, PhD, CEng, FIMarEST
Jeff Hawksley, a retired marine engineer, is a LTVAS member who has concentrated on industrial history. He was a major contributor to the LTVAS book *The Mills & Waterways of Romsey*. More recently, he has played the key role in unravelling the design story behind Berthon's collapsible boats. His hobby is making meticulous woodwork models from scratch, and examples of his work are in Romsey Heritage Centre.

Recollections from other people include contributions from Captain Sir Thomas Barlow, Miss Kay Bowen, Vice Admiral Sir Louis Le Bailly (connected to the Berthon family by marriage), Mr Michael Rea (donor of the Berthon boat in Unst Heritage Museum), Mrs Louise Stewart Cox (née Berthon), Mr Richard Whiting, Mr Nevil Harvey Williams (great-grandson of Captain Frederick Harvey) and Mr A.V. Yearsley.